*The Superior Person's Second Book
of Weird and Wondrous Words*

# The
# *Superior Person's*
# Second Book of
# Weird and Wondrous
# Words

BY

*Peter Bowler*

## Illustrated by Ron Bell

DAVID R. GODINE, PUBLISHER
BOSTON

First U.S. edition published in 1992 by
David R. Godine, Publisher, Inc.
Horticultural Hall
300 Massachusetts Avenue
Boston, Massachusetts 02115

Library of Congress Cataloging-in-Publication Data
Bowler, Peter.
The superior person's second book of weird and wondrous words
/ by Peter Bowler ; illustrations by Ron Bell.
p.    cm.
ISBN 0-87923-928-X
1. Vocabulary.   2. English Language—Glossaries,
vocabularies, etc.   1. Title
PE1449.B636   1992                     92-7750
428.1—dc20                     CIP

*First edition*
PRINTED IN THE UNITED STATES OF AMERICA

TO DI, WITH LOVE

## *Unbalanced Lexicographer Does It Again!*

This is grim news indeed for all lovers of the English language. The deranged lexicographer Peter Bowler, whose 1985 book *The Superior Person's Book of Words* did more damage to the cause of serious language studies than the information technology industry and the colleges of advanced education combined, has escaped from his confinement in ultramontane bureaucracy and has inveigled a sensation-seeking publisher into releasing this further collection of his verbal *curiosae* upon an unsuspecting public.

The six hundred new words included herein are just as outlandish as the five hundred in the previous volume, the definitions just as idiotropian—indeed, if anything, even more so. What more can we say? Regrettably, it has to be admitted that there are people out there who will want to buy this book for the worst possible reasons—to inflate their already excessive self-esteem, to humiliate their unlovely friends and relatives, to complete their valueless collections of Bowleriana. To them we say: Why not buy three copies? And to those other, nobler spirits who, like the present reader, will seek elevation and instruction within these pages . . . for you we have nothing but admiration. Sorry about that.

# Exordium

When, some ten years ago now, I wrote *The Superior Person's Book of Words*, I little dreamed that it would have such a formative influence upon the world of belles lettres and project management. Now, of course, it is as familiar a sight in the nation's bookstores and newsstands as Wittgenstein's *Tractatus Logico-Philosophicus*, and widely conceded withal to be the more amusing of the two works. Its presence in our schools, where sniggering English teachers find it even more effective a stupefier for their rebarbative students than *Middlemarch* or *The Bridge of San Luis Rey*; its popularity with intellectual parvenues and persons wishing to give their employers and relatives a Christmas present of a faintly insulting nature; its apparent attraction for antisocial adolescents; all these evidences bespeak the universality of its appeal. I have indeed received several "fan" letters from enthusiastic readers, though, sadly, none has as yet accepted my courageously candid invitation to send money.

All this, it seemed to the good people at David R. Godine, amounted to an irrefragable (q.v.) case for the issue of a sequel. Especially in the light of the precedents set recently in a sister medium by *Jaws II*, *Superman II*, and of course the paradigm of the genre—*Return of the Living Dead II*. Hence the present volume, which in the fullness of time will, I trust, come to be seen as the *Return of the Living Dead II* of philology.

The format and the objectives are the same as before. I wish to equip the person in the street with new and better verbal weapons—words that would otherwise lie unseen and moribund in the smallest print of the largest dictionaries. To give my reader, so to speak, a fuel-injected, turbo engine for the language that they speak, so that they may the more readily assert a fitting ascendancy over their fellows at the traffic lights of life.

But enough of such flights of fancy. It is time for me to lay before you a second compilation of definitions of unusual and distinctive words. As before, I have taken the liberty of including some jeux d'esprits and even one or two deliberate errors. Stay awake.

*Peter Bowler, 1992*

# Ex-odium

To a reader as discerning as yourself, the following probably goes without saying, but just to leave no doubt at all in anyone's mind: The personal names appearing in this book are not those of real people, but are mere figments of the author's fevered imagination, dredged up from his resupinate subconscious for illustrative purposes only.

*The Superior Person's Second Book*
*of Weird and Wondrous Words*

# ❧ A ❧

**ABDABS** or **HABDABS** *n.* ❧ A state of extreme nervousness. The jitters. One of those marvellous, naturally expressive terms which the dictionaries don't even try to etymologize. "Hoo-ha" is another. "All this hoo-ha is giving me the abdabs."

**ABLIGURITION** *n.* ❧ Extravagance in cooking and serving. "So wise of you to have chosen Mabel, Reginald. Abligurition is such a comforting thing in a fiancée."

**ABSQUATULATE** *v.* ❧ To leave in a hurry, suddenly, and/or in secret. "No problems, Mr. Burbage; just make the check out to cash—I'm doing the accounts tonight and you can rely on me to absquatulate first thing in the morning."

**ABSTRICT** *v.* ❧ To set free spores by constriction of the stalk. Not a common activity, in the literal sense, but the term has obvious figurative possibilities.

**ABSUMPTION** *n.* ❧ The process of being wasted away or consumed, e.g., as food scraps in a compost heap, flesh in the grave, etc. "So this is your twentieth year in the civil service, Jeremy? You must be qualified for absumption by now."

**ACEPHALOUS** *a.* ❧ Without a head. Condition of a "Project Team" in a government department which is implementing an "Industrial Democracy Mission Statement." Also that of a decapitated fowl.

ACESCENT *a.* ❧ Turning sour. "It's a rather wonderful thing, darling, but as we grow old together it seems to me that you are, if possible, even more acescent than ever."

ACETABULUM *n.* ❧ The cup-shaped sucker of a cuttlefish or similar marine tentacle-flourisher. "Get home before midnight, don't crash the car, and don't let that superannuated pinball parlor groupie friend of yours get her acetabula on your already overextended credit cards!"

ADUMBRATE *v.* ❧ To foreshadow in general terms; to sketch out what you intend to do, or what you expect to happen. "Allow me to adumbrate in general terms the consequences of your continuing to block my driveway . . . "

ADVENTITIOUS *a.* ❧ Accidentally intruding from an unexpected quarter. "How adventitious, madam, that you should reverse your car into the very space occupied by my own!"

ADVOWSON *n.* ❧ The right to identify the clergyman who will hold a particular benefice, or church living. The nearest thing today to this quintessentially eighteenth-century Episcopalian power would be that of our party political powerbrokers in the preselection of electoral candidates and the pasturing out of faithful party hacks to the available sinecures.

AFFENPINSCHER *n.* ❧ A breed of small dog, related to the so-called Brussels griffon, and having tufts of hair on the face. A young man growing a beard for the first time could be referred to in casual conversation as being in his affenpinscher phase. ("So-called," incidentally, is a particularly useful adjective, implying as it does *without actually saying so* that there is something not quite kosher about the noun to which it is attached. After all, the Brussels griffon *is* so-called—because it is a Brussels griffon. Can you imagine it being *not* so-called, when that's what it is? "And now, ladies and gentlemen, let's hear it for our so-called Congressman!")

AILUROPHILE *n.* ❧ Someone who is abnormally fond of cats. Such a one may readily be identified by the fleas and fine hairs hovering in the air like an aura about their person. Be kind to them; they have probably just spent a small fortune on canned fishwaste.

ALPHAMERIC *a.* ❧ Made up of letters and numbers. The astute reader will at once deduce that this new word, already in use, is actually a compression of *alphanumeric,* a term encountered sooner or later by all who use personal computers. "During this term, Robert made giant strides forward in his handwriting, which is now almost alphameric."

AMICUS CURIAE *phr.* ❧ Literally, a friend of the court (i.e., court of law). A disinterested party whose advice assists the court. Given the high cost of justice these days, perhaps a more apposite modern meaning would be "investment adviser."

ANACREONTIC *n.* ❧ A poem the tone of which is amatory and convivial. Interesting in that the only words which rhyme with it (pontic, odontic, gerontic, mastodontic, and quantic) are all equally or even more obscure in meaning—thus affording you the opportunity to compose some fairly daunting verses for the next meeting of your local poetry group. Quantic, for example, means "the rational integral homogeneous function of two or more variables." Need I say more?

ANADROMOUS *a.* ❧ Ascending rivers to spawn. Obviously a term from the realms of ichthyology, but none the less one with its uses in other contexts—for example, to characterize those among the beautiful people who believe that a Jacuzzi is the proper place for sexual congress.

ANFRACTUOUS *a.* ❧ Intricate or circuitous. "Sit down, Wilbur. I realize that you are wondering why we have decided to fire you, and I want you to know that I intend to give you the most anfractuous explanation possible."

ANGLOPHONE *n.* ❧ A speaker of English. No—not a communication device for fishermen. It probably says something Toynbeeesque about the life cycle of civilizations that most anglophones are now anglophobes, whereas most francophones are still francophiles. (Besides, how many words can *you* think of with three successive "e"s?)

ANIMADVERT *v.* ❧ To pass a critical comment, or animadversion, upon something or someone. The term was more neutral in its original sense of a judicial recognition or reference. Thus, having said "If you will allow me to animadvert upon your recent conduct, Richard," and after a suitably foreboding pause, you could, strictly speaking, come out with a pontification that was perfectly bland.

ANIMUS *n.* ❧ Commonly used these days to mean animosity, i.e., hostility; but more properly animating spirit, mind, soul, or life force. "I have listened to the last speaker's animadversions with great equanimity, since I am fully aware, as I think all of us are, that underlying his criticisms there is no animus whatever."

ANTANAGOGE *n.* ❧ A countercharge made in retort to an adversary's accusation. "It ill becomes you, Penelope, to cavil at another's alleged action in eating the rest of the chocolate turtles when, if you will permit me to lodge an antanagoge, you yourself were the only person present last Wednesday when

an entire packet of sherbet and marshmallow cones
disappeared overnight."

ANTEDILUVIAN *a.* ❧ Literally, before the flood; but commonly used to mean incredibly old-fashioned. As a reader of this book, you are more than likely to be regarded by your children as antediluvian—but you may take comfort from the fact that, until they buy their own copy, they will
be unable to tell you so.

ANTHROPOMORPHISM *n.* ❧ Attribution of human characteristics to what is not human. "Are you serious? Cousin Henry on the electoral roll? My God! How far can anthropomorphism go?"

APATETIC *a.* ❧ Imitative in color or shape. A term from the world of zoology but obviously adaptable to that of human fashion. Or, for that matter, to that of *psephology* (q.v.). "Splendid idea to run for Congress, Simeon; who more than you to appeal to the apatetic vote?"

APOSTATE *a.* ❧ Guilty of abandoning one's faith or principles. The possibilities for juvenile paronomasia with this one ("I hear he's having trouble with his apostate," etc., etc.) are too obvious for me to refrain from mentioning them.

ARCIPLUVIAN *a.* ❧ Many-colored (literally, like a rainbow). Perhaps the right adjective for today's commuter cyclists—the ones who dress themselves up for their diurnal velocipedal progressions to and from the office in the multihued, iridescent, skintight Spandex uniform of the Tour de France rider. Most of these luminous apparitions are not hypnagogic hallucinations, but account clerks.

AXIOPISTY *n.* ❧ The quality that makes something believable. "The trouble with Alvin is that he has no axiopisty."

AZOIC *a.* ❧ Lifeless. Technically, this is a geo-historical term referring to the era before life first appeared on earth; but there is no reason why you should not apply it in a metaphorical sense to the condition of your teenage daughter's bedroom on Sunday morning before the noontide *expergefaction* (q.v.).

## ❧ B ❧

BALLADROMIC *a.* ❧ Maintaining a course toward an ultimate target. "Look out the window. See—there at the end of the street? That's young Jimmie coming home from school. Now see the container on the kitchen table here? That's the frosted caramel slices. Now watch the path he follows. See? Turns right and crosses the road diagonally; passes the oleanders on the left but swerves to pass the power pole on the right. Pure economy in movement. Balladromic from start to finish."

BANDOLINE *n.* ❧ A strong-smelling unguent for the hair, said by my sources to be made from boiled quince pips. This seems intrinsically implausible, but it is the function of the lexicographer to record the form of his subject matter, not examine its substance. Still . . . quince pips? *Why* quince pips?

BATHYCOLPIAN *a.* ❧ Deep-bosomed. "So you're both Baptists, eh, Ernest? Well, I guess I'm a lapsed Catholic— but my wife is bathycolpian."

BESHREW *v.* ❧ Another of those quaint archaisms which the Superior Person delights in using for their intensely irritating effect on the listener. "Beshrew me, if it isn't old Arthur!" Literally, beshrew means "curse," but the general effect of "beshrew me" is "the Devil take me"—or perhaps, in more vulgar parlance, "bugger me," or its stronger variant "bugger me dead." In all these instances, of course, the speaker's utterance is metaphorical, not literal, in intent.

BEZONIAN *n.* ❧ A rascal, scoundrel, or beggar. "Of course I'll take a couple of your raffle tickets, Mrs. Oliphant. Heavens, I don't know what the school would do without you; you are a true bezonian!"

BICRURAL *a.* ❧ Having two legs. "I am sorry to have to say this in front of the boys, headmaster, but I have come to regard you as bicrural, and I cannot be persuaded otherwise."

BILOCATION *n.* ❧ Being in two places simultaneously. A difficult achievement, one would think, except in the case of the *consubstantial* (q.v.), and the fourteen-year-old human male, who has been reliably reported as having one hand in the fridge and one in the pantry in real time.

BIOLUMINESCENCE *n.* ❧ The generation of light by living organisms. Metaphorically speaking, one of the functions of the lexicographer.

BIRL *v.* ❧ To revolve a log in the water while standing on it. I knew it—there just had to be a word for it. We've all seen it done at the movies or on television—and now you and I know what it's called. This is powerful information. Chances are you will never meet *anyone* else who knows what this word means. Use this knowledge wisely.

BISTABLE *a.* ❧ Having two stable states. "My husband is bistable—when he's asleep and when he's unconscious. Unfortunately he's unconscious only on Friday nights."

BLABAGOGY *n.* ❧ Criminal environment. "Taking 3B again for Personal Development Studies, Carruthers? How is it affecting you—working in a blabagogy every day?"

BLENNOPHOBIA *n.* ❧ A morbid dread of slime. "I'm so sorry, Clifford, I know mother told you that she thought I'd love to go out with you, but the fact is I have this medical thing at the moment, this blennophobia, and I'm afraid that rules out a date with you for the foreseeable future."

BOMBILATE *v.* ❧ To make a humming, buzzing, or droning sound. BOMBILATION: the sound made by a well-meaning father trying to show he is "with it" by singing along with your Led Zeppelin tapes in the car.

BOOBOISIE *n.* ❧ The slower classes; the stupid masses. A term coined by H. L. Mencken. The more savage American writers—Ambrose Bierce, Phillip Wylie, Mencken, and the like—seem to have a gift for what one might term neo-invectivism, another example of which is Wylie's MICROPOOPS, for pinheaded paperpushers.

BORBORYGM *n.* ❧ The noise made by gas in the bowels. Yes, a fart. "Mom, Quentin's doing Work Experience in Social Welfare Studies this term. He goes round a different suburb every Thursday afternoon leaving borborygms in phone booths."

BOTHAN *n.* ❧ A booth or hut, more especially one that is used as an illegal drinking den. "Do you have to turn the toilet into your personal bothan, Miles?"

BOTTOMRY *n.* ❧ A type of mortgage under which a ship is put up as security for a loan to finance its use in a freight-carrying venture. Sometimes also referred to as "bummery." I swear I am not making this up. "I know you've always wanted to join the merchant marine, son—but swear to me that you'll never, never resort to bottomry."

BOVARISM *n.* ❧ A magnified opinion of one's own abilities. An affliction manfully borne by most of us (including the author, whose abilities have nonetheless patently fallen short of coming up with a nonsexist alternative for "manful").

BRADYKINETIC *a.* ❧ Moving very slowly. Alternative sense: one who jumps up dynamically to switch off the TV when *The Brady Bunch* comes on.

BRASH *n.* ❧ As a noun, this has nothing to do with rude self-assertiveness but means, as the Concise Oxford coyly puts it, "an eruption of fluid from the stomach." Yes, folks, this is yet another euphemism for "vomit." "Set up the next round of drinks, fellers! *Beshrew* (q.v.) me if I'm not just going outside for a brash; and then I'll be with you."

BRATTICING *n.* ❧ A board fence around something dangerous. "There we are, Mrs. Lebowitz; a little work on the hemline, a tuck or two around the waist, a little bratticing around the bodice, and you'll be ready to roll."

BREASTSUMMER *n.* ❧ Believe it or not, this beautiful word denotes the beam supporting the upper front part of a building, over its main door or portico. "Ah, Mrs. Sandalbath, as I came in I admired your breastsummer so much. What a superstructure!"

BRIMBORION *n.* ❧ Something useless or nonsensical. "I thought you'd really appreciate a little brimborion," you can shyly say to your friends and relatives when you give them their Christmas present—a copy of this book.

BROMIDROSIS *n.* ❧ Smelly perspiration. Osmidrosis means the same thing. "Do I *have* to sit with one of the Connolly brothers, Mom? What a dilemma—it's like being caught between Osmi and Bromi . . . what's that, Mom? . . . oh, just a classical allusion."

BUNDOBUST *n.* ❧ Arrangements, organization. (From the Hindi *band-o-bast,* meaning "tying and binding.") Surely a good trading name: The Bundobust Moving and Storage Company.

BYSSUS *n.* ❧ A high-quality fabric used for wrapping mummies. Oh, all right then—your mother's beach towel.


## ❧ C ❧


CABALLINE *a.* ❧ Horselike. "Just turn your head to the right a little, Miss Montmorency, while I set the focus and shutter speed. I want to have the light falling on you in half-profile, to bring out that . . . how shall I describe it? . . . caballine quality in your facial structure . . . "

CACHINNATE *v.* ❧ To laugh loudly or immoderately. "It's not that I don't like bridge, dear, or that I object to your friends occupying the den all afternoon. It's the cachinnation that I find a little hard to take."

CACODAEMON *n.* ❧ A malignant spirit. (Alternatively, *cacodemon,* but the diphthong is always to be preferred—orally as well as in written form.) "And now . . . it is my privilege, as Student Council President, to introduce to this Speech Night audience someone who for many years has been the school's veritable cacodaemon—our Vice Principal!"

CAMBIST  *n.*  One who is skilled in the science of financial exchange. A teenager on weekly-allowance day. "But I mowed the lawn *and* bagged the grass clippings, and you owed me that other two dollars from the week before last, and you said three weeks ago that you'd give me three dollars for munchies at the movies, and although I didn't go then I will be going next week, and remember I paid the bus fare last Wednesday out of my own pocket, and I needed to get that magazine to read at the dentist's, and a month ago when I went to the store to get milk and you said I could keep the change and I forgot and left it on the kitchen table, and . . . "

CANESCENT  *a.*  Tending to white, hoary. One of that useful class of words which permits honesty without discourtesy when treating the subject of another's personal appearance. To the hearer, ignorance is bliss.

CAPARISON  *n.* or *v.*  Commonly used these days (well, of course it's *not* commonly used, but you know what I mean) in the sense of a rather grand form of attire, or to dress someone in rich attire. The interesting thing is that the original meaning was simply the covering for a horse—a piece of information that may afford you some quiet satisfaction at an appropriate time. "You are indeed magnificently caparisoned tonight, Lady Smoothe-Lewis."

CAPRICIOUS  *a.*  Fickle, whimsical. As you well know. But were you aware that the derivation is from the Latin *caper*— a goat? "When I say that our distinguished guest tonight is capricious, I hope he will realize that I am not using the term in its modern sense, but in the original sense, which of course is quite different. This is borne out by his whole career, in the union movement, in the courts of the land, and in Congress . . . "

13

CARRACK *n.* ❧ A large ship of burden, which was also fitted for fighting. This may, but only may, be a good description of some readers' mothers, mistresses, or spouses.

CARUNCLE *n.* ❧ A small, fleshy excrescence. When you are *really* annoyed by a short person: "Sir, you are nothing but a caruncle!"

CASTROPHENIA *n.* ❧ The belief that one's thoughts are being stolen by enemies. A condition much to be preferred over *nastrophenia,* the belief that one's thoughts are not worth being stolen by enemies.

CATACHRESIS *n.* ❧ Misapplication of a word. In using the lore and learning contained in this book, you will undoubtedly be found guilty of this. In your defense, you can at least say *(a)* that you are aware of your lapse, and *(b)* that you know what it is called.

CEPACEOUS *a.* ❧ Like an onion. "So this is your new boyfriend, Imelda! I can tell just by looking at him that he's your type—same eyes, same cepaceous head . . . "

CHAETIFEROUS *a.* ❧ Bearing bristles. Also CHAETIG-EROUS and CHAETOPHEROUS. If your boyfriend *must* start growing a beard, at least you ought to know what to call him.

CHALYBEATE WATER *n.* ❧ A mineral water, supposedly impregnated with iron, for consumption as a pleasant and restorative tonic. One of those gorgeous late Victorian terms like "mucilage." You took the air at Brighton and you had your chalybeate water afterward. Do what you can to revive this word. Ask the checkout girl at the local supermarket where you can find their chalybeate waters.

CIRCUMAMBAGIOUS *a.* ❧ A roundabout or indirect manner of speech. Not as effective, perhaps, on the whole, as an aid to obfuscation, as the sesquipedalianism fostered by this book, always assuming, if you will forgive a somewhat Jamesian digression (Henry, that is to say, in contradistinction to P. D.) that obfuscation is in fact the objective, and having in mind also that, setting aside the relative merits of the two different approaches toward that end, vis-à-vis each other, it can hardly be doubted that the employment of both together, as distinct from one or the other, must have a still greater obfuscatory, or perhaps more precisely, obscurantist, impact, a point well evidenced by the fact that this particular instance of circum-ambagiousness, aided by only the merest hint of sesqui-pedalianism, has, as I believe you will discover, successfully diverted your attention from the fact that nowhere in this ad-mittedly now somewhat overlong sentence is there, despite its superabundance of subsidiary clauses, a principal subject or verb.

CIRCUMFUSE *v.* ❧ To pour, spread, or diffuse around. "Well, I've dug up the ground, I've fertilized it, and I've raked it level—but some other lout can circumfuse the bloody lawn seed." Always a good idea to juxtapose the vernacular with the sesquipedalian whenever possible. (For "sesquipedalian," see— that means, *buy,* cheapskate—this book's predecessor, *The Superior Person's Book of Words.*)

CLINOMANIA *n.* ❧ Excessive desire to stay in bed. Not a bad mania, as manias go; and a reasonably plausible excuse for taking Monday off.

COCCYX *n.* ❧ What you fall on when your feet slip forward from under you, as when wearing thongs on moss-covered mud. The small triangular bone at the bottom of the spinal column, called "coccyx" because it is shaped like the bill of a

*kokkux,* or cuckoo. "Please, Miss, I've hurt my coccyx—
will you have a look at it for me?"

COCKALORUM *n.* ❧ A self-important little man. (From
"High Cockalorum," a game said to be not unlike leapfrog.
The exact nature of this game is unknown to the present author,
but it could conceivably be that known to the
present age as "Politics.")

COMMENSAL *a.* or *n.* ❧ Eating together; one who eats
with another. Normally used in a technical sense, referring to
the habits of animals and plants, but, figuratively, a nice term
for a dinner companion. "I say, waiter—would you mind
sponging down the curry spillage on my commensal?"

COMPLORATION *n.* ❧ Wailing and weeping together.
"Your mother coming over this Christmas, darling,
for the usual comploration?"

COMPOTATION *n.* ❧ A drinking party. "Wayne's just in
his first week at university, and they're having all these traditional ceremonies—matriculation and orientation, and he says
that every night they have what they call compotation . . . "

CONSUBSTANTIAL *a.* ❧ One of those words from the
wonderful world of magic and myth (see *obsolagnium*) which
describe entities or states that are supposed to exist even though
there is no hard empirical evidence for their existence. In this
case, consubstantial means "having the same substance or es-
sence"; yet it is said of *different* beings, i.e., beings that are not
the same. So the use of the term implies a belief that things
that are different are in fact the same. The classic use of the
term is in Christian theology, to describe the Trinity. There
may be other uses. "Now listen closely, children. Two weeks
after buying himself a state-of-the-art compact disc player, with
amplifier and speakers, valued conservatively at $1,250, your

father has bought your mother, for her birthday, an ovenproof casserole dish. Imagine that! Liberality and lousiness combined in the one being! Your father is the living proof of consubstantiality!"

CONTRECTATION *n.* ❧ The act of caressing someone furtively or against their will. "So that's agreed. We'll begin by asking each candidate about their educational qualifications and their skills in relation to the selection criteria—communication, management, finance, contrectation, and so on—then we'll . . . "

CONTRUDE *v.* ❧ To push, thrust, or crowd together. At the line at the post office, ask permission to contrude before making your forward move; there's always the chance that someone who doesn't know what it means will concur.

CRIME PASSIONEL *phr.* ❧ (From the French.) A crime motivated by the passions—such as the murder of a treacherous lover. As with other foreign or classical terms (see *pinus radiata*), the Superior Person always uses the original pronunciation—in this case, for example, "crime" is pronounced as "cream." At the average dinner party, there is always at least one guest who is not familiar with the phrase and can be persuaded, while the hostess is out of the room, that crime passionel is in fact the name of the passionfruit cream dessert that has just been served. This can lead to some entertaining after-dinner conversation.

CUCKING STOOL *n.* ❧ A chair in which disorderly women were, in olden times, ducked in the water as a form of punishment. In even more olden times, a cucking stool was something like a commode, since to cuck was to defecate. The word is ugly enough to be revived for use in American films and other vehicles for the rebarbative.

# ❧ D ❧

DANDIPRAT *n*. ❧ A silly little fellow or urchin. Nothing to do with "dandy," but from the French "dandin," i.e., a ninny or simpleton. Your young nephews and grandchildren will *hate* being jovially addressed thus, even if they haven't the faintest idea what it means—especially if you can manage to pat them on the head at the same time.

DAPATICAL *a*. ❧ Sumptuous (as of a feast). "I hope you'll be patient with me tonight, Samantha; I find that since I got underway with my low-cholesterol diet, I can't properly enjoy a meal unless it's dapatical."

DASYPHYLLOUS *a*. ❧ Having crowded, thick, or woolly leaves. Applying a little *anthropomorphism* (q.v.) to this, one could so characterize your typical skiers, geared and kitted out like multi-hued astronauts for their day in the snow.

DEBLATERATE *v*. ❧ To babble. "Right—no more apologies, and the minutes of the previous meeting confirmed? Okay then, on to Agenda Item One, and let the deblateration commence!"

DEGLUTITION *n*. ❧ Swallowing. "If you're really serious about losing weight, Mrs. Hallibutt, we'll have to do something to reduce your deglutition count."

DELTIOLOGY *n*. ❧ The collecting of postcards as a hobby. "In support of my application for the position of Executive Director, I should mention my skills in human resource management, deltiology, communication . . . "

DEMERSAL *a*. ❧ Sinking to the bottom, as for example certain fish eggs, or babies whose New Age mothers think it would be lovely to teach them to swim at the age of three months.

DEMOPHOBE *n.* ✤ A person who has a morbid dread of crowds and massed humanity. Condition of most of us during the pre-Christmas shopping period. One of the most common of phobias; if all the sufferers were put together in one place, they wouldn't like it one bit.

DENDROPHILOUS *a.* ✤ Attracted to or living in trees. The correct epithet for militant save-the-forest conservationists, especially those who chain themselves to trees or pole-sit in the branches overhead.

DENTILOQUY *n.* ✤ The act or practice of talking through clenched teeth. Ventriloquists are almost, though not completely, dentiloquists. "Really, dear, do we *have* to have the dentiloquy bit again? Just because of a *tiny* scratch or two on the hood—which wasn't all my fault anyway? I mean I was concentrating on reversing—how was I to know that you'd left the toolbox on the car roof?"

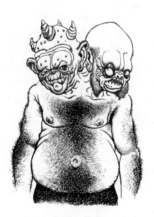

*Derodidymus*

DERODIDYMUS *n.* ❧ A two-headed monster. "My God, she's bringing the twins with her! Derodidymus alert! Warning, warning, derodidymus alert!"

DESIPIENT *a.* ❧ Silly, trifling, or foolish. "How marvelous that you're enrolling your daughters with us, Lady Fubwell! The school cherishes these traditional family links. And tell me—dare we hope that they will be as desipient as you were, in your day?"

DEUCED *a.* or *adv.* ❧ Exceeding(ly), devilish(ly). "This is deuced civil of you, old man" is a pleasantly deflating response to an unwanted courtesy. The derivation is as ambiguous as the term itself. Said to be from "deuce," the low-scoring two in a dice game, and hence the devil of a result from your throw; but some derive it from the Old French "dieus" or "gods."

DIAMANTIFEROUS *a.* ❧ Yielding diamonds. "I don't care what you say—I still prefer Julian. Craig may be younger and more handsome, and unmarried for that matter; but Julian is diamantiferous."

DIASKEUAST *n.* ❧ One who prepares material in detail. A researcher, editor, et al. Even a lexicographer.

DIDAPPER *n.* ❧ One who disappears and then pops up again. From "dive" and "dapper" (a variant of "dipper"). Specifically applied to the dabchick, a small freshwater diving bird. Or, perhaps, a teenager between mealtimes.

DIDYMITIS *n.* ❧ Not something you'd wish on your worst enemy. Unless, of course, he didn't know what you were talking about. Inflammation of the testicles.

DIMEROUS *a.* ❧ Consisting of two parts. Confronted by your hostess with The Perfect Couple, you undermine her faith in their perfection by whispering, "Ah, yes, but have you not heard—their marriage is a dimerous one."

DIOESTRUM  *n.*  ❧ The time during which a female animal is not in heat. "This is Jenny's father speaking, Craig. We expect her dioestrum to occur tomorrow afternoon about 3:00 P.M. and to last till about 3:45 P.M., so you'd be very welcome to drop in during that time if you wish."

DISCALCED  *a.*  ❧ Bare-footed. "O.K. if I go to church discalced this morning, Mom? It's an old Carmelite tradition, according to Father Ryan."

DISCISSION  *n.*  ❧ Sticking a needle into the eye. A surgical term, which you yourself are unlikely to have occasion to use; but as well to know the meaning, just in case your ophthalmologist nonchalantly uses the word while casually discussing your next eye test.

DISCONTIGUOUS  *a.*  ❧ Not touching, or even near. "It is my dearest wish to be completely discontiguous to the Honorable Senator . . . "

DISEMBOGUEMENT  *n.*  ❧ A discharging at the mouth, as of a stream. "No, Mrs. Davenport, the Bulgarian cold cabbage and radish soup was delicious, absolutely delicious! It's just that I need to use the bathroom for a moment. A necessary disemboguement, you understand."

DISSAVE  *v.*  ❧ Believe it or not, this delightful word means exactly what it ought to—the opposite of "save." To dissave is to spend more than one's income by drawing upon one's savings or capital. In a sense, it could be said that the ultimate object of all saving is dissaving; this is something that not many people realize.

DIVERSIVOLENT *a.* ❧ Looking for trouble or argument; seeking out a divergence of view. "Dearly beloved, we are gathered together here in the sight of God, and in the face of this congregation, to join together this Man and this Woman in Holy Matrimony, duly considering the causes for which Matrimony was ordained. First, it was ordained for the mutual society, help, and diversivolence that the one ought to have of the other . . . "

DIVULSION *n.* ❧ Rending asunder; being torn apart. "Would you care for a little divulsion after dinner, dearest?"

DOLORIFUGE *a.* ❧ That which relieves or drives away sadness. A *viscerotonic* (q.v.) innamorata, for example.

DOXOGRAPHER *n.* ❧ A compiler of opinions of philosophers. Domestic scene: "You know what *I* think?" "Hold everything! Call the doxographer, children! Your father is about to express an opinion!"

DOXOLOGY *n.* ❧ Hymn of praise to the Almighty. The Greater Doxology is the *gloria in excelsis* and the Lesser Doxology the *gloria patri*. When, at close of day, you are greeted by your spouse with a statement of the Achievements of the Day, you may wish to expostulate: "Bravo, my dear! Now— would you prefer the Greater or the Lesser Doxology?

DRACOCEPHALIC *a.* ❧ With a dragon-shaped head. Choose your own uses for this word. But be careful; you are not the only person to have bought this book.

DRAPETOMANIA *n.* ❧ Intense desire to run away from home. Unaccountably, there doesn't appear to be a word for that much more common condition—an intense desire for someone *else* to run away from home.

DRESSAGE  *n.* ❧ The training of a horse in obedience and deportment. The thought that a human being, particularly an upper-class female human being wearing jodhpurs and a bowler hat, can train a horse, of all creatures, in deportment, must be one of the more laughable conceptions ever given credence by the otherwise sober pages of a dictionary.

DYSLOGY  *n.* ❧ Dispraise; uncomplimentary remarks. The opposite of "eulogy." "Okay, everyone, let's hear it for the retiring President! Let's give him the dyslogy he so richly deserves!"

DZIGGETAI  *n.* ❧ A kind of wild ass, rather like a mule. "And this is my young brother Jason. He's a regular little dziggetai now that he's taken up *tae kwon do,* aren't you, Jason?"

## ❧ E ❧

EBRIECTION  *n.* ❧ Mental breakdown from drinking too much alcohol. "I hope you won't have an ebriection like my previous two bosses, Mr. Palethorpe."

ECDEMIC  *a.* ❧ Originating elsewhere than where it is found. "These children we keep finding in the kitchen now that Damien has started school . . . I've only just realized that even though their appetites are omnipresent they themselves are ecdemic."

ECDYSIS  *n.* ❧ The shedding of a snake's skin. "Ah, the first warm days of spring! I'll have to change to short-sleeved shirts soon—and for you, dear, the time of ecdysis must be approaching."

*Ecdysis*

·EFFLORESCENCE  *n.* ❧ Do not for a moment consider that your having long since left school absolves you from the responsibility for remembering, and distinguishing between, the meanings of this word and its host of friends and relatives. Now concentrate. *Efflorescence:* flowering or (in chemistry) crystallization. *Effervescence:* bubbling. *Deliquescence:* liquefaction. *Inflorescence:* floral structure of a plant. *Infloration:* inflorescence. *Defloration:* dehymenization. *Defervescence:* reduction in heat or fever. *Refervescence:* resurgence of heat or fever. Sorry; there's no refloration.

EFFLUVIUM  *n.* ❧ An intangible emanation or exhalation. Normally taken now to imply an unpleasant odor, but originally a hypothesized medium to account for magnetic attraction and repulsion. Or, in the elegant words of *Dr Gregory's Portable Encyclopaedia Comprehending The Latest Improvements in Every Branch of Useful Knowledge,* published in 1826: "a term much used by philosophers and physicians, to express the minute particles which exhale from most, if not all, terrestrial bodies in the form of insensible vapors." Try not to be too cruel in the use of this word when commenting upon the extent to which your various acquaintances are nice or otherwise to be near.

ELAPIDATION  *n.*  ❧ The clearing away of stones. A process commonly applied to the front yards of newly built homes, the kidneys and gallstones of the middle-aged, etc. But wait—there is a second, quite different, meaning here. In zoology, the elapids are the front-fanged snakes—the ones with the venom. So the elapidation of your neighbor's front yard could involve not only clearing it of stones but also strewing it with cobras.

ELDRITCH  *a.*  ❧ Weird or hideous. "In concluding my report as President on the year just concluded, I want to make special mention—and I know the Committee joins with me in this—of our eldritch member, Mrs. Porringer, who . . . "

ELECTUARY  *n.*  ❧ A medicine that is licked up, as distinct from being eaten, drunk, inhaled, injected, or absorbed. Usually made by incorporating the medicinal ingredient in a doughy or pasty mass. "And now, ladies and gentlemen, the speaker you have all been waiting for—our own local Congressman, whom I am sure you will welcome as befits your chosen . . . er . . . electuary."

ENCEPHALALGIA  *n.*  ❧ Headache.  But "encephalalgia" will look better on a sick-leave application, won't it?

ENCHIRIDON  *n.*  ❧ Handbook. "I admire your new car, Gregory, but I'd pay close attention to the enchiridon if I were you."

ENCOPRESIS  *n.*  ❧ Unintentional defecation. "Hope it goes well for you at your big performance tonight, Benedict! When that curtain rises and the spotlight falls on you—here's wishing you lots of applause, excitement, and all the encopresis in the world!"

ENDOPHASIA *n.* ❧ Inaudible speech. "You've got only two alternatives once you get into that witness box, Simon—perjury and endophasia."

ENGASTRATION *n.* ❧ Stuffing one bird inside another. I don't explain the definitions; I only report them.

ENGASTRIMYTH *n.* ❧ Ventriloquist. Alternatively, a tall story about how many toasted bagels you ate last night during the horror film marathon. "And what would little Susie like Mommy and Daddy to hire for her birthday party? A prestidigitator or an engastrimyth?"

EPIGAMIC *a.* ❧ Attractive to the opposite sex. Presumably it is a manifestation of the divine sense of humor that so many who are homosexual are also epigamic.

EPIPHRAGM *n.* ❧ A secretion which a snail uses in dry weather to seal its shell and protect itself from drying up. The gel which your daughter's boyfriend applies to his hair on Saturday nights.

EPISTEMOPHILIA *n.* ❧ An abnormal preoccupation with knowledge. The curse of the lexicographer.

EPURATION *n.* ❧ A purge, as of officials suspected of treachery. "Another promotion for Cyprian! He's done well in the civil service, hasn't he, Maree? What will be next? A department of his own, do you think, or epuration?"

EREMOPHILOUS *a.* ❧ Inhabiting a desert. Condition of someone who has bought a newly built house and then been confronted by the classic choice between having curtains and having a lawn.

ERUCTATION *n.* ❧ A belching forth. Can be applied, as by Virgil, to the eruption of a volcano, or to the eruption of rashly consumed foodstuffs or gases from the human alimentary tract. See *polyphagia.*

ESCHATOLOGY *n.* ❧ The study of the Four Last Things— presumably the opened packet of rice crackers, the salami end, the kiwi-fruit marmalade jar, and the sachet of no-brand de-hydrated noodles at the back of the bottom shelf.

ESCHEAT *n.* or *v.* ❧ A property that returns to state own-ership, e.g., for want of an heir or through confiscation. To so reacquire or confiscate property. (An *encheat,* incidentally, is the revenue from an *escheat.*) Nothing to do with cheating. Unless . . . classroom teacher to the boy in the back row, as she seizes the *Treasure Island Classics Comic* from which he has been cribbing during the exam: "You cheat; I escheat."

ESCHEW *v.* ❧ To abstain from. In the preceding example, the precocious pupil might reply with a plea for the escheater to eschew escheating.

ESCULENT *a.* ❧ Fit to be eaten. "Ah—as always at your table, Lady Hyperno—nothing in any way esculent tonight, I see. How on earth do you do it?"

EUGONIC *a.* ❧ Living on artificial foodstuffs. Strictly speaking, this refers to bacteria being bred in a laboratory, but clearly the term is applicable also to the male teenager with the fast-food fixation.

EUMOIROUS *a.* ❧ Lucky or happy as a result of being good. A term not commonly encountered. 'Nuff said?

EUMORPHOUS *a.* ❧ Well-formed. "Ah, the eumorphous Miss Mullins! Come in, my dear, come in!"

EXFOLIATE *v.* ❧ To remove layers of skin, scales, or similar surface laminations one after the other. "Would you care to exfoliate your Christmas presents now, Deborah?"

EXOPTABLE *a.* ❧ Extremely desirable. "The next item on the Agenda is New Members. I think we might call on Miss Perkins to stand and read out the list of candidates. Does everyone agree that Miss Perkins is exoptable?"

EXORDIUM *n.* ❧ A beginning or preamble to the written or spoken treatment of a subject. Not to be confused with "exodium"—the conclusion of a drama or the farce following it. Or with "ex-odium"—absolved from blame, without fault. Sermons traditionally begin with the exordium and end with the exhortium. After which comes the exodus.

EXOTERIC *a.* ❧ Intelligible to outsiders, i.e., not esoteric. "I can read you like a book, James; you are totally exoteric."

EXPERGEFACTION *n.* ❧ An awakening. "Action stations! Action stations! Eight forty-five A.M., and I am about to perform expergefaction upon your mother!"

EXPISCATE *v.* ❧ To examine or discover skillfully. Your purchase of this book constitutes an act of supreme expiscation.

❧ F ❧

FABIFORM *a.* ❧ Bean-shaped. "And I'd like you to meet Brett and Wanda, and their children Jamie and Cass—round here we call them the Fabiform Four."

FACUNDITY *n.* ❧ Eloquence. Not to be confused with fecundity, i.e., fertility. (But, rather wonderfully, pronounced the same way.) "Pray silence for our next speaker, Mr. Spinelli, who will give us a demonstration of his impressive facundity."

FAFF *v.* ❧ To dither or fumble (about). This delightful word offers the genteel alternative to "farting about" that you've all been looking for. "Stop faffing about, for heaven's sake, and get in the car."

FANFARONADE *n.* ❧ Arrogant bragging or boasting, particularly in introducing something. "The next item, ladies and gentlemen, will be little Cheryl Peabody playing *The Sparrow's Parade*. But first—can we have the usual fanfaronade from Mrs. Peabody?"

FANNY ADAMS *n.* ❧ According to both Oxford and Chambers, Sweet Fanny Adams was a famous early-nineteenth-century victim of murder and dismemberment, and hence "Sweet F. A.," a reference to something previously existent but now nonexistent. Readers who may have long believed that the acronym "F. A." stood for something entirely different now have an excellent justification for its use in civil discourse.

FANTABULOUS *a.* ❧ A hybrid word meaning "fantastic and fabulous." A similar, more recently coined hybrid is "humungous," meaning "monstrously huge or portentous." Such coinages are generally found to be in vogue with the callower and flashier members of our society, and tend to be, mercifully, short-lived. They ordinarily reflect a tendency to hyperbolize, and hence are particularly common among public relations officers and salespeople. A printer's representative who called upon the author recently at his place of work, to lodge her firm's quote for a particular printing job, lost all hope of credibility for the said quote when she assured him as she left that it had been "fabulous" to meet him.

FARCEUR *n.* ❦ Strictly speaking, an actor or writer of farces, but in common parlance a wag or humorist whose japes lean toward the practical. Thus the young Barry Humphries, whose Melbourne exhibition of dada art is said to have included a pair of boots filled with custard and labelled "Pus in Boots," could be so described.

FARRAGINOUS *a.* ❦ Having the characteristics of a farrago, i.e., a hotchpotch or disordered mixture. Normally one speaks of a farrago of lies, or of half-truths, but there is nothing intrinsically mendacious about the farraginous; nor is farraginosity necessarily a characteristic only of statements (in theory, one could speak of a farrago of dirty linen on a teenager's bedroom floor). "A truly farraginous effort," you could say of your Chairperson's preliminary summation of the issues.

FARTHINGALE *n.* ❦ A hoop skirt or dress distended by whalebone or crinoline. The term dates from as early as the sixteenth century but may still be used to pleasing effect, whether in referring to mid-fifties rock-and-roll attire, which appears to be undergoing something of a revival, or to some aspect of your sister's party dress (should you wish to ostensibly compliment but actually unsettle her). Incidentally, for the benefit of any pedants *manqué* who are wetting their pants with impatience to take me to task for the expression in the preceding parenthesis, allow me to inform you that there is no such thing as the so-called "split infinitive."

FARTLEK *n.* ❦ Okay, here's one for my juvenile readers. Nothing amuses a thirteen-year-old so much as the word "fart." But "fartlek" has nothing to do with the evacuation of bodily gases. (Did you know, by the way, that the average adult releases one liter of gas per day? Imagine what a senior politician must do to the ozone layer!) Fartlek, for those who are still paying attention, is a method of training long distance runners, whereby the trainee runs across country, alternating speed work with slow jogging. From the Swedish, meaning, literally, "speed play." Why not call out from the back of the class, during a quieter moment: "Miss Adamson, do you know what Smith does every Thursday afternoon after school? He does *fartlek!* For two hours!"

FEBRIFUGE *n.* ❧ Something that reduces fever. A cooling drink. To be confused—as far as possible—with "centrifuge," a spinning machine to separate liquids. "Excuse me a moment, Reverend Coot; I just need to pop into the laboratory and put some alcohol in my febrifuge."

FERETORY *n.* ❧ A shrine for relics carried in procession. A good name for that small receptacle built into the dash of your spouse's car, just beneath the stereo, where repose the torn scraps of ancient shopping lists, the packet of digestive tablets with just one left, the broken pencil stub, and the crumpled ball of used tissue. "How should *I* know where the video membership card is—have you looked in the feretory?"

FITCHEW *n.* ❧ A polecat, or kind of carnivorous weasel—and one described by the O.E.D. as "fetid" (i.e., stinking) to boot. Not a nice creature. A good name perhaps for a politician who is elected on a platform which he or she proceeds to betray as soon as he or she is in office. Come to think of it, a good name for any politician.

FLABELLATION *n.* ❧ The use of a fan to cool something. Nothing to do with flab, but everything to do with flabella, a fan. "And now, my best beloved," you whisper to your *viscerotonic* (q.v.) innamorata, "would you care for a little flabellation?"

FLAGITIOUS *a.* ❧ Grossly criminal, utterly disgraceful, shamefully wicked. Perhaps the ultimate in condemnatory adjectivism. Not even a *fitchew* (q.v.) descends to the flagitious. Well . . . not on a good day, at any rate.

FLOCCULENT *a.* ❧ Covered with soft woolly tufts. Condition of a male teenager's face.

FLUBDUB *n.* ❧ A glorious nineteenth-century word meaning "bombastic language." Use it together with "flimflam" (humbug, idle talk). "Did you hear the Message to the Nation last night? All flimflam and flubdub, as usual."

FORFICULA *n.* ❧ Small shears or scissors. The Superior Person's word for nail scissors.

FOUMART *n.* ❧ Heavens, another name for a polecat! Though this one sounds, perhaps, a little less unpleasant than *fitchew*. Perhaps a foumart could be a politician who betrays the platform on which he or she is elected, *and then ashamedly resigns*. But wait . . . there aren't any of those, are there?

FRIPPET *n.* ❧ A frivolous female show-off. Not to be confused (though, let's face it, most of us do during this life) with a "poppet," or dear little girl. And *certainly* not to be confused with a "frisket," which is the iron frame of a hand press.

FUBBERY *n.* ❧ Cheating, deception. From "fub," meaning "fob" as in "fob off"—to put someone off with a slightly dodgy story or excuse. "Enough of your fubbery, my good man! Tell me exactly what the total price is, including *all* on-road costs!"

FUCOID *a.* ❧ Like seaweed. "And how would madam like her hair styled today? Bouffant perhaps? Or an impish gamine effect? Or perhaps *très* fucoid, *comme maintenant?*"

FUNAMBULIST *n.* ❧ A tightrope walker. "Political candidate requires qualified funambulist for full-time public relations officer position."

FUSTIGATE *v.* ❧ To cudgel, i.e., to beat with a stick. "Don't worry, lady—you can safely leave little Fido in our kennels for the holidays. We feed them, we exercise them, we brush their coats, and we fustigate them daily."

## ❧ G ❧

GABION *n.* ❧ A bottomless basket of earth, used in fortifications and engineering. Do I hear you cry: What use is a bottomless basket of earth? One can only presume (the privilege of the lexicographer, who by definition has no actual expertise in anything at all, let alone fortifications and engineering) that today's gabion is one of those huge iron buckets which are seen dangling from the ends of cranes and disgorging their contents when a lever is pulled to open up their bottoms. Be that as it may, there are obvious alternative uses for the term on the domestic scene. The cardboard carton that you fill with garden rubbish and which then comes apart underneath as you carry it to the corner, dumping wet compost and rose clippings on your good suede shoes. The plastic shopping bag that tears open and deposits your six giant-size glass bottles of soft drink on the concrete footpath—but not until you have got *just* far enough away from the supermarket to make it unrealistic to contemplate going back there to complain. The brown paper bag containing your lunch which you inadvertently place on the one wet spot on the table and which later chooses to give way just as you step off the footpath, dropping your salad sandwiches squarely in the gutter. These are the gabions of our time.

GALEANTHROPY *n.* ❧ The delusion that you have become a cat. Not a *particularly* common disorder, but its mere existence compensates, at least in part, for the fact that so many cats suffer from the delusion that they have become humans.

*Galeanthropy*

GALIMATIAS *n.* ❧ Nonsense, gibberish; confused and meaningless speech. "And now for our final speaker. Roderick is, as you all know from the panel discussion earlier, a consultant in educational management and someone who is well versed in the theory and practice of galimatias. Tonight his subject is 'Managing Lifelong Education for Articulation Along Its Vertical or Longitudinal Dimension.'"

GALLIVANT *v.* ❧ To gad about, especially with members of the opposite sex. To roam in search of pleasure. A lively word for a lively activity. ("Gad," incidentally, comes from an Old English word meaning "good fellowship.") Prepare little cards to leave on your front door, saying "Gone Gallivanting"; let your unwanted visitors know what kind of a person they're dealing with.

GAMBRINOUS *a.* ❧ Full of beer. From Gambrinus, a mythical Flemish king who was supposed to have invented beer. "Don't worry, darling; while you're away I swear I'll be totally gambrinous."

GAMOPHOBIA *n.* ❧ A morbid fear of marriage. Clinical psychiatrists bear a heavy burden, knowing as they do, when treating a phobia, that the cure may be more fatal that the disease.

GERONTOCOMIUM *n.* ❧ An institution for the care of the aged. You could at least *try* this one on Grandpa; he might think it's a new kind of condominium.

GIMMACES *n.* ❧ Chains used in hanging criminals. "Yes, Garth, your new gold chain *does* show off your tanned chest very nicely—but somehow I feel you'd look even better in gimmaces."

GLEBOUS *a.* ❧ Full of clods. The amenities room at your office during the lunch hour.

GLOBOSE *a.* ❧ Spherical. Pronounced with the accent on the "bose." It seems, somehow, less hurtful to refer to an obese acquaintance as "globose" than as "globular," doesn't it?

GLYCOLIMIA *n.* ❧ A craving for sweets. "Robert, before you leave those frosted caramels on the kitchen table, please take cognizance of the fact that you are in the presence of your younger sister, a registered glycolimiac, and that I take no responsibility for her actions after sundown."

GNATHONIC *a.* ❧ Obsequious, toadying, parasitical, flattering, deceitful. Yes, all of these at once. From Gnatho, a character in Terence's *Eunuchus*. A good one to use in written

35

references for Upwardly Mobile Young Managers, who certainly won't know what it means and are unlikely to be able to find out. "Andrew has a pleasant manner, presents well, and has been responsible for the introduction of Mission Statements and Output-Related Performance Indicators in this Department. He has been consistently gnathonic, especially when under pressure, maintaining good relations with senior management and . . . etc., etc., etc."

GOODPASTURE'S SYNDROME *n.* ♣ Pneumonitis with haemoptysis followed by glomerulonephritis and uraemia. Thanks a bunch, Goodpasture.

GOSSOON *n.* ♣ A young lad. Somehow the term seems to have connotations of well-intentioned brainlessness. Useful for alienating the offspring of unwelcome relatives, etc., by using it in unwantedly avuncular remarks: "Well, Cousin Henry—and how are your young gossoons these days?" (Also goes well with a pat on the head.)

GRAMINIVOROUS *a.* ♣ Grass-eating. Perhaps a passable, if slightly unfair, epithet for your vegetarian acquaintances. "And could my friend see your graminivorous menu, please?"

GRAPHOLAGNIA *n.* ♣ A fascination for obscene pictures. "Well, Reverend, I've been at art school for a year now, and it's been the making of me. I think I enjoy the grapholagnia most of all; it's not as practical as industrial design, of course, but then personal satisfaction is so important too, isn't it?"

GREMIAL *a.* ♣ Pertaining to the lap or bosom. As a noun, according to Chambers, "the cloth laid on a bishop's knees to keep the oil off his vestments during ordinations." As usual, Chambers excites our interest and then leaves us in some uncertainty. Why *knees,* when "gremial" refers to laps and bosoms?

Do bishops not have laps or bosoms? Is oiling a bishop's bosom more acceptable than oiling a bishop's knees? And just what exactly is going on at these so-called "ordinations," anyway? Perhaps we should set such considerations aside, and merely note that you could quite properly refer to a table napkin as a gremial, especially given its alternative placings—upon the lap or tucked in at the neck.

GRIFFONAGE *n.* ❧ Careless handwriting; illegible scribble. When you've picked up your prescription from the doctor and you're paying the receptionist, don't forget to ask if there is a charge for the griffonage.

GROBIANISM *n.* ❧ Rudeness, boorishness. "Heavens, how did you manage to bring up the children to such a perfect state of grobianism? My husband's been working on ours for years but never seems to get anywhere."

GYMNOPHOBIA *n.* ❧ Fear of nudity. But—fear of *whose* nudity? One's own or someone else's? And what has this got to do with gymnastics? And why?

GYNEPHOBIA *n.* ❧ Morbid dread of the company of women. "Desirée, I need your help. The psychiatrist thinks that I'm cured of my gynephobia, but there are certain tests that he feels I must successfully undergo before he can finally pronounce me well again. Now, for these tests I need the assistance of someone such as yourself . . . "

GYNOTIKOLOBOMASSOPHILE *n.* ❧ Someone who likes to nibble on a woman's earlobe. Truly, there is a name for everything. This one is reported in the amazing dictionary of verbal exotica compiled by Mrs. Josefa Heifetz Byrne (the daughter of Jascha Heifetz, incidentally). One for the Personals: "Gynotikolobomassophile wishes to meet woman with large ears."

GYROVAGUES *n.* ❧ Monks who were accustomed to wander from place to place. In modern times, perhaps, any of the various circumforaneous proselytizers who go from door to door—Jehovah's Witnesses, Mormons, et al.


## ❧ H ❧

HABROMANIA *n.* ❧ Extreme euphoria. "Of course, after my first wife died, I went through a period of profound habromania . . . "

HALIEUTICS *n.* ❧ Fishing. "No, I can't claim any great expertise in nonparametric statistics, and I realize their relevance to the selection criteria. On the other hand, I have some twenty years' experience in halieutics, and I'd be looking to build further on that if I were to get the job."

HALITUS *n.* ❧ Exhalation, breath. Easily confused with "halitosis," or bad breath. A few of us may have halitosis but *all* of us have halitus. "Your halitus is a little strong this morning, Reverend; you haven't been out jogging again, have you?"

HAPTODYSPHORIA *n.* ❧ The shiveringly unpleasant feeling experienced by some people when they touch certain surfaces, such as peaches or wool. "Yes, I *know* Roger plays jazz piano and earns $100,000 a year; but I can't help it, he just brings out the haptodysphoriac in me."

HARMATIOLOGY *n.* ❧ That part of theology which deals with sin. "So little Sharon is doing Divinity this year! That must be very gratifying for you, Mrs. Mulholland—and she'll be doing her work experience in harmatiology, then?"

HEBDOMADAL *a.* ❧ Weekly. (The Hebdomadal Council of Oxford University is a representative board that meets weekly.) Surprise the next office management group meeting by suggesting that it is not really necessary for the group to meet hebdomadally.

HERDWICK *n.* ❧ A pasture for cattle or sheep. "Off to the herdwick again, old chap?" you jovially enquire of your civil servant neighbor as he sets off for work in the morning. A nice effect can be obtained with this word by pronouncing it "herrick," which is quite inauthentic
but *deuced* (q.v.) plausible.

HESTERNOPOTHIA *n.* ❧ A pathological yearning for the good old days. You know—when World War II was in full swing, your children got diphtheria, and dentists used slow drills and no anaesthetic.

HETEROMORPHIC *a.* ❧ Having different forms at different stages of the life cycle. As for example the caterpillar/butterfly. Or your friend Marion, who goes to the office on Friday in her Dragon Lady With Full Make-Up form and then appears in her back yard on Saturday in her Jumpsuit And Thongs Without Make-Up form.

HETERONYM *n.* ❧ A word having the same spelling as another, but a different pronunciation and meaning. To be distinguished from a homonym, which is a word with the same pronunciation as another but a different spelling. Then of course there's a homograph, which is a word with the same spelling *and* pronunciation as another but a different meaning. Enliven the after-dinner conversation by brightly asking: "Can a word be a homonym of its own heteronym, and if not why not a homograph?"

HIERODULE  *n.* ❧ Temple slave. "When I am engaged in creative cuisine, oh my beloved, this kitchen is my temple and you my hierodule. So wash the dishes!"

HIPSANOGRAPHER  *n.* ❧ Someone who writes about relics. "Well, if you really can't find anyone to ghostwrite your mother's stupid memoirs, why not look up 'hipsanographers' in the phone book?"

HODIERNAL  *a.* ❧ Of or pertaining to the present day. "Do not have any doubts on this score, Arabella; my love for you is hodiernal."

HOPLITE  *n.* ❧ A heavily armed foot-soldier of ancient Greece. The word "panoply," meaning an impressive array, derives from *pan hopla,* i.e., the full armor of a hoplite. Who are our modern hoplites? American football players, perhaps? Skateboarders? Ice hockey players? Fencers? Not at all. "Back, cursed hoplite!" you might well cry through your open car window at the commuter cyclist who appears beside you at the traffic lights, with his bulbous helmet, his luminous multicolored knee-length Spandex tights, his orange Day-Glo knee and elbow protectors, and his canary yellow stormproof backpack.

HORNSWOGGLED  *a.* ❧ What Popeye is by the actions of Brutus. Repeatedly so. "I's bin hornswoggled!" is the doughty little sailor's constant complaint as he is hurled into the air, the water, the nearest brick wall, etc. From the ancient maritime practice of the same name. Though why the term should be applied to the doings of characters who appear to be members of the United States Navy is not entirely clear. (It was, of course, *British* seamen who traditionally hornswoggled each other.)

HORRISONANT *a.* ❧ Sounding terrible. Your neighbor's cornet practice; your son's rap records; almost any modern so-called "serious" music; and the piano music of Scott Joplin.

HUGGERMUGGER *n., a., adv., v.t.* or *v.i.* ❧ This grammatically chameleonic term denotes secrecy, clandestine activity, muddle, and/or confusion—generally all at once. A useful synonym for "Executive Management Team Meeting." The author admits to a weakness for such double-barrelled colloquialisms: "argle-bargle" or "argy-bargy," meaning a dispute or wrangle, and "arsy-versy," meaning topsy-turvy. Come to think of it, all these terms relate pretty well to the Executive Management Team Meeting.

HUMICUBATION *n.* ❧ The act or practice of lying on the ground—more especially in penitence or self-abasement. Some potential uses: *Bank robber*: "Humicubate, or die!" *Advertisement in the Personals*: "Gretel—in your home or motel—bondage and humicubation." *Superior Person*: "No, Roger, I am not intransigent; all I expect from you is a little humicubation."

HYGEIOLATRY *n.* ❧ Fanaticism about health. More useful, these days, would be a word for fanaticism about *fitness*—an increasingly prevalent condition, judging by the thousands of goggle-eyed whirling dervishes of our time bounding about in aerobics classes and jogging their way doggedly around what, but for their presence, would be scenic tracks and pathways.

HYPAESTHESIA *n.* ❧ Diminished power of sensation or sensitiveness to stimuli. (Alternatively "hypesthesia," but no reader of this book would, I trust, ever use "e" where they could use "ae.") "I don't suppose you'd want to come to the concert tonight, Simon? Not with your hypaesthesia, poor dear?"

HYPERHEDONIA *n.* ❧ A condition in which abnormally heightened pleasure is derived from participation in activities which are intrinsically tedious and uninteresting. For a case study near you, see any golfer.

HYPOBULIA *n.* ❧ Difficulty in making decisions. The real difficulty for most of us, of course, is in making the *right* decisions; but, typically, there doesn't appear to be a word for that.

HYPOGEAL *a.* ❧ Pertaining to, or occurring in, the earth's interior. A journey by underground railway might be described as hypogeal—as might the daily parking of your car in the subbasement level of the office parking lot.

*Hypogenous*

HYPOGENOUS *a.* ❧ Growing on the under side of anything, as for example a fungus on the underneath of a rock. "Wash those bare feet of yours this instant, young man! You've already introduced enough hypogenous life forms into the carpet to keep a team of microbiologists busy for a month!"

HYPONYCHIAL *a.* ❧ Under the fingernails or toenails. "Sorry to hear the naturopathic herbal treatment's not working, Mavis. Have you thought of trying hyponychial acupuncture?"

HYPOTHIMIA *n.* ❧ Profound melancholy or mental prostration. State of a householder whose electricity bill and rates notice have arrived in the same week. Useful for sick leave applications, combining as it does an element of truth about the applicant with a vague suggestion of contagious skin eruptions, thereby serving to keep one's colleagues at work at and indeed beyond arm's length.

## ❧ I ❧

ICK *sf.* ❧ The Superior Person should be alert not only to the *conversational* potential of words and word-forms but also to their potential for *written* use. A nice effect can be obtained by the addition of the archaic "k" to otherwise uninteresting "ic" suffixes. Thus "comick," not "comic"; "physickal" (or, better still, "physickall"), not "physical"; "garlick," not "garlic." Mind you, like the garlick itself, this little device should be used sparingly. Once per missive, at the most. You want to gain a reputation as a lovable eccentric, not a laughably bad speller.

IDIOGLOSSIA *n.* ❧ A secret language invented by children, or a psychological condition in which speech is so distorted as to be unintelligible. "Ixnay on the ermonsay, Dad!; your idioglossia's more potent than ours."

IGNIS FATUUS *n.* ❧ Will-o'-the-wisp, i.e., the elusive lights generated by marsh gas at night and likely to lure incautious travelers from their path. Literally, "fool's fire." Observing Jason and Priscilla arrive, arm in arm, at the party, you whisper to your companion: "Ah, the fatuous and the *ignis fatuus.*"

ILLUMINATI *n.* ❧ People who have, or claim to have, exceptional intellectual or spiritual awareness. Add to these the cognoscenti, the literati, the luminaries . . . why are there so many of these and so few of us?

IMMORIGEROUS *a.* ❧ Unyielding, inflexible. "No way am I immorigerous!" you might shout, over and over again, hammering at the table to emphasize the point, your expression brooking no denial.

IMPAVID *a.* ❧ Fearless, unafraid. Condition of a Hell's Angel during a confrontation with a lexicographer.

IMPERCUSSIVELY *adv.* ❧ In a manner free from percussion. After a cursory inspection of the family car's paintwork, you jovially exclaim to your spouse: "Ah, I see that you drove impercussively today, my beloved."

INCONVENANCE *n.* ❧ Impropriety. The accent is on the "con," which helps to avoid confusion with "inconvenience"—always assuming, of course, that you *wish* to avoid such confusion. "Madam, for your sake, no inconvenance would be too great."

INDOCIBLE *a.* ❧ Unteachable. "Can't understand why you should have any trouble with 3B, Cartwright. I've always found them utterly indocible."

INFUNDIBULAR *a.* ❧ Why say "funnel-shaped" when you can say "infundibular"

INGEMINATE *v.* ❧ To repeat or reiterate. "At the risk of offending Mrs. Suddaby, I will now ingeminate."

INGRAVESCENT *a.* ❧ Growing worse. A medical term relating to the course of a disease, but the wider figurative potential is obvious. "Now that he's elected to office, we can expect him to be ingravescent, I'm afraid."

INNASCIBLE *a.* ❧ Without a beginning. God; the circumference of a circle; and the fame and fortune of a lexicographer.

INOSCULATE *v.* ❧ To unite by mouths or ducts. (Or, one assumes, mouths and ducts.) "Shall we inosculate, dearest? Your mouth, my duct? Or vice versa this time?"

INSENSATE *a.* and INSENTIENT *a.* ❧ The meanings are related but not identical. *Insensate* means without sensitivity or humane feeling, whereas *insentient* means inanimate, i.e., *incapable* of sensitivity, humane feeling, or indeed awareness. Thus, only a sentient being can behave insensately. "I'm sorry I attacked Pillburn with such intense rage, Headmaster, but I did so under the impression, based on his behavior over a whole term, that he was insentient."

INTERBASTATION *n.* ❧ Evoking as it does an impression of some unseemly form of sexual congress, this word could be useful for the disturbing of maiden aunts—especially since the actual meaning is "quilting."

*Interbastation*

45

INTERMITTENT *a.* ❧ Literally, placing between; but of course in common use as meaning "coming and going" or "on and off"—as for example the lowest setting on your windshield wiper switch. This otherwise commonplace phrase is included here because of the inventive way in which it is used by Oliver St. John Gogarty in *Rolling Down the Lea:* "Inarticulate sounds of inattention" [from the person to whom Gogarty was speaking] "told me that I was talking to an intermittent mind."

INTEROCULAR *a.* and INTEROSCULAR *a.* ❧ It is quite important to get these right. *Interocular* means between the eyes (as in the case of some insects' antennae) or within the eye (as in ophthalmic surgery); *interoscular,* on the other hand, means mutual kissing, a different thing entirely. *Oscular* by itself means kissing. In fact, come to think of it, what difference can there be between *oscular* and *interoscular?* If it's *oscular,* it presumably must be interoscular—unless your lips are so protuberant that you can kiss yourself. But such things are beyond the province of pure lexicography.

INTERSILLENT *a.* ❧ Suddenly emerging in the midst of something. "I'd ask you round to my place tonight, Rory, but my little brother Wilbur is at home, and he's so intersillent."

INTESTACY *n.* ❧ The state of not having made a will. "Have you heard about poor Arthur's intestacy? I suppose he won't be able to have children now."

INTROJECTION *n.* ❧ The absorption into one's very self of beings from the outside world, so as to experience oneness with them. "I don't mind your damned dogs in themselves, but with all those bloody fleas the possibility of introjection is something I don't want to even think about."

INTROMITTENT *n.* ❧ Literally "putting something into" —more technically, something which has the capacity to be put into, specifically in the context of the reproductive processes of biological organisms. Birds and bees stuff, this . . . need I say more? A reference to your "intromittent part" could be introduced into polite conversation with your young lady without necessarily giving offense.

INTUSSUSCEPTION *n.* ❧ The taking in of foreign matter by a living organism; or the inversion of one part of an intestine, or similar organic tube, into another. Useful, perhaps, to describe your adolescent children's eating habits. And a guaranteed stumper for smart-aleck know-it-alls in spelling competitions.

INURBANE *a.* ❧ Not urbane. There are both metaphorical ("uncouth") and literal ("rural") meanings here; seize every opportunity to confuse the two. "I think it would be probably fair to say about Charlie that, whilst he's . . . inurbane, I don't think it could be said that he's . . . inurbane."

INVULTUATION *n.* ❧ The act of sticking pins into a wax doll to cause pain and injury to a particular person whom the doll is designed to represent. "Well, dear, let's see. You've tried naturopathy, homeopathy, and iridology, and they don't seem to help. The only option left would seem to be invultuation; would you like me to arrange a little of that for you?"

IRREFRAGABLE *a.* ❧ Not refragable. Or, if you are so *pernickety* (q.v.) as to require a fuller definition—unbreakable. Normally used of argument or evidence. Something that is incontestable, i.e., cannot be gainsaid. (To gainsay something is to against-say, or contradict, it). Note that in litigation an irrefragable bank balance always wins out over an irrefragable case.

IRRESPONDENCE *n.* ❧ Lack of respondence, failure to reply. Typical irrespondents are nieces, nephews, debtors, appliance service centers, prospective employers, government offices, and literary agents. "And to my dear relatives, in return for twenty years of irrespondence, I bequeath my pens, envelopes, embossed stationery, staplers, and rubber bands."

❧ J ❧

JACULIFEROUS *a.* ❧ Possessing spines like darts. Suitable epithet for a punk hairdo.

JARGOGLE *v.* ❧ To befuddle or mess up. "Congratulations, dearest; I wouldn't have thought it possible, but you've found something else to jargogle."

JAR-OWL *n.* ❧ The European goatsucker. I swear that this is the complete definition as given by my source. Goatsucker? Do not write to me or to the publisher to explain this. Neither of us wishes to know.

JEOFAIL *n.* ❧ A mistake made by a lawyer and acknowledged as such by her to the court. There appears to be no comparable word for a mistake made and acknowledged by a judge; but then, when a lawyer becomes a judge, as everyone knows, she ceases to make mistakes.

JOLLOPED *a.* ❧ Equipped with a jollop, or fowl's dewlap. A nicely jovial term for references to double chins. "More jolloped than ever, I see, Henry—good to see!"

JUBATE *a.* ❧ Fringed with long, hanging hairs, such as a mane. "I see that you've become even more jubate with the passing years, Willoughby—have you achieved Rastafarianism yet—or are you aiming for full equinization?"

JUMENTOUS *a.* ❧ Pertaining to the smell of horse urine. So says the dictionary. But what could possibly *be* pertaining to the smell of horse urine? And how could it so pertain? Is this word really necessary?

JUVENESCENT *a.* ❧ Becoming youthful. An extraordinary word, when you think of it. After all, no one does this. Why should there be a word for it?

# ❧ K ❧

KAKORRHAPHIOPHOBIA *n.* ❧ The morbid fear of failure. Imagine a sufferer reporting to the clinic for treatment, knowing that the first thing he will have to do, at the reception desk, is give them the name of his complaint. Think about it.

KALOKAGATHIA *n.* ❧ A condition or state in which the good and the beautiful are combined. The author's natural modesty precludes his revealing at this time the identity of the only true kalokagathical in our society; but the general absence of the condition in the community at large should not deter you from making some use of the term in polite discourse, for example in ironic references to those who most noticeably do *not* possess the condition. "Not a very kalokagathical sight," you might observe wearily, as a panting IRS official, naked from the waist up, jogs effortfully past you at the lakeside during your lunch hour.

KALOPSIA *n.* ❧ A state in which things appear more beautiful than they really are. Presumably love.

KAMALAYKA *n.* ❧ A waterproof shirt made from the entrails of seals. You may think not many people would be that anxious to be waterproof. But no doubt it helps the market for entrail-proof undershirts.

KAMICHI *n.* ❧ The horned screamer (a South American bird). "And this is my wife Kay—though her friends and I have an affectionate little Japanese nickname for her—Kamichi."

KIBE *n.* ❧ A nice, short, simple word. Should be more like it. My dictionary defines this as meaning "a chilblain, especially on a heel." "Medical report for Sixth Battalion, sir: ten men with chilblains—no, make that nine men with chilblains and Major Featherbed with kibes . . . " Why "chilblain"?, I hear you ask. From "chill" and "blain"— the latter being a boil or blister.

KIPPAGE *n.* ❧ Commotion, confusion. "Rest assured, Mrs. Foskit, that little Jimmy will be completely safe on the school excursion. We don't just put them on a bus and cross our fingers, you know; we have teachers who are especially trained in kippage skills to go with them."

KLIEG LIGHTS *n.* ❧ The interesting thing here is not the meaning (you all know klieg lights are those ultrabright arc lights used on movie sets etc.) but the derivation. They are named after the Kliegl brothers, who invented them. So, in the unlikely event of your ever having to mention Klieg lights in casual conversation, why not use the pronunciation "Kleegle"? After the inevitable argument, that should effectively confirm your growing reputation as a scholar and a nut-case.

KRATOGEN *n.* ❧ The dormant area of land lying next to one which is prone to earthquakes. "And this is the main bedroom. We've had this double bed for twenty years now, ever since we were married. Oscar sleeps on that side, and I sleep here on this side, which I call the kratogen."

KROTOSCOPE *n.* ❧ An applause-measuring instrument. Surely a two-edged sword worthy of comparison with the magic mirror on the wall in *Snow White,* in that those who have the greatest hunger for its readings are those least likely to be satisfied by them.

# ❧ L ❧

LAABA *n.* ❧ A storage platform high enough to be beyond the reach of animals. (An Alaskan word.) Also, the top shelf of the pantry, where the kids can't get at the animal-shaped gingersnaps and the packets of colored cake sprinkles.

LABEFACTION *n.* ❧ Shaking, weakening, and/or downfall. "Not in *Who's Who* yet, Carstairs? Even after three years in Congress? Never mind—those who deserve labefaction always achieve it in the long run."

LAEVOROTATORY *a.* ❧ Counterclockwise. A useful alternative for "widdershins" (see *The Superior Person's Book of Words*) when your family and friends finally work that one out. "What do you mean, how do you turn it on? It's a tap, child, a tap—laevorotatory, laevorotatory, of course."

LALLATION *n.* ❧ Unintelligible baby talk. "Denise, I *must* introduce you to Sandra. You two talk the same language—I know you'll get on marvelously. Stand back, everyone, and let the lallation begin!"

LANCEOLATE  *a.* ✤ Shaped like a lance-head—about three times as long as it is broad, and tapering more gently toward apex than base. Sound like any of your friends?

LANGUESCENT  *a.* ✤ Becoming tired. Somehow the languidity implicit here bespeaks an altogether superior form of tiredness—a world-weariness, perhaps, brought on by the sheer profundity of your reflections upon the late-night party scene from which you grow impatient to depart. "Alas, Sybil—time for me to go now; languescence has set in, I'm afraid."

LAPACTIC  *a.* ✤ An aperient, or laxative. "What would you like for starters, Colonel? Whisky, gin, soft drink . . . something lapactic, perhaps?"

LAPILLUS  *n.* ✤ A tiny pebble thrown out by a volcano. "And what lapillus can we expect to emerge from the ferment of your mighty intellect tonight, Herr Doktor?"

LATEBRICOLE  *a.* ✤ Living in holes. Or, if you prefer, in what modern town planners and urban managers increasingly refer to as "medium density residential facilities."

LATIBULIZE  *v.* ✤ To hibernate. Function of a teenager during that part of the morning when papers are being brought in, cats being fed, garbage cans put out, digital clocks being reset after overnight power failures, etc., etc.

LATIFUNDIAN  *a.* or *n.* ✤ Rich in real estate. "If you *must* be multicultural and marry an ethnic person, Lavinia, for heaven's sake be realistic and choose a latifundian."

LAY FIGURE  *n.* ✤ It is important to understand that this is not the same as "layman," i.e., nonprofessional or nonclerical. A lay figure is a jointed wooden figure of the human body, used by artists for draping material on. Hence it has come to mean an unimportant person or nonentity, or a fictional character who has not been realistically fleshed out. "Well, we've heard what the experts think about it. Now let's have the views of a lay figure. Gilbert?"

LENITIC *a.* ❧ Living in quiet waters. The aspiration of the *kakorrhaphiophobiac* (q.v.) lexicographer.

LEPID *a.* ❧ Charming, elegant, amiable. While watching your butterfly-hunting cousins gassing and impaling their catch for the day, you could perhaps engage them in light conversation, in the course of which you might express genteel surprise that lepidopterists are themselves so rarely lepid.

LESTOBIOSIS *n.* ❧ Living by furtive stealing; specifically a feature of the ant world in which two species live side by side and one lives by furtively stealing the food collected by the other. Nonplus the kids with this one when they're having their usual fight over the ownership of a packet of chips.

LIBRATE *v.* ❧ To oscillate, or swing from side to side. "No use asking Adrian; put a simple question to him and he goes into a libration frenzy."

LIGNICOLOUS *a.* ❧ Growing on wood. "Short back and sides for the young fellow, Mrs. Paramore? Always best when the hair is lignicolous."

LIMICOLOUS *a.* ❧ Living in mud. "Looks like those limicolous Kingsley kids are on the way over—better get the hose out."

LIMOPHOITOS *n.* ❧ Insanity brought on by lack of food. A condition occurring in older teenagers after about ten o'clock at night, causing them to do strange things after the rest of the family have gone to bed, such as eating eight slices of cheese on toast while watching rap videos.

LINGULATE *a.* ❧ Tongue-shaped. "The doctor said my tongue was lingulate, and there wasn't anything he could do about it—then started laughing. Do you think it's wise to keep on going to him?"

LINONOPHOBIA *n.* ❧ Morbid fear of string. Not much of a problem these days, I would think. Now, if you had a morbid fear of bar codes, you'd be in big trouble.

LOGANAMNOSIS *n.* ❧ A mania for trying to recall forgotten words. Do you remember "lethologica"—inability to recall words—from this book's predecessor? Well, you wouldn't, would you, if you suffered from it. But in any event the present word goes rather beyond that; loganamnosis is the compulsive perseverance of a lethologiac to summon up that elusive memory—that maddening word that's "on the tip of my tongue." Most people give up after a few minutes; the loganamnostic reduces himself or herself to a neurotic case study in the attempt. And of course, as we all know, it's only when you finally stop trying to remember that you suddenly do remember. Another example of the divine overseer's sense of humor.

LOGORRHEA *n.* ❧ Excessive and incoherent talking. "Who on earth can we seat next to Mrs. Maudsley? And in any case—is logorrhea contagious? Would it be safer to put her at the foot of the table?"

LOGOTYPE *n.* ❧ Never say "logo." The Superior Person always uses the full rather than the shortened form, the original rather than the modernized.

**LONGANIMITY** *n.* ❧ Suffering in silence over a period of time, while brooding on revenge. "That's O.K., Mom; I accept your decision with complete longanimity."

**LORICATE** *a.* ❧ Having a hard, protective crust or shell. "Are you going to go to the Simpsons' barbecue without makeup, or fully loricate?"

**LUCTIFEROUS** *a.* ❧ Sad and sorry. Suggested conclusion for your primary school homework essay: "And so we all returned, luctiferous, from our day at the beach." Primary teachers use only *The Typist's Pocket Dictionary, Simplified Version,* so she'll never find out what you meant.

*Lumbricoid*

**LUDIFICATION** *n.* ❧ Derision. "Why not send some of your poems in to the paper, darling? Do you good to get a little ludification."

**LUMBRICOID** *a.* ❧ Like an earthworm. "I respect your aspirations as a bodybuilder, Gilbert; but as a lover you're just too lumbricoid."

**LUPANARIAN** *a.* ❧ Pertaining to a brothel. "Sorry, Reverend, but Billy just feels he's a little too old now for the Boy

Scouts. But if it's any consolation, he's thinking of becoming a lupanarian."

**LURDANE** *a.* ❧ Dull and lazy. "Ritchie's results this term were every bit as good as might have been hoped. His lurdanity seems, if anything, to grow with the years—something few of us would have thought possible."

**LUTULENT** *a.* ❧ Muddy, thick, or turbid. A good word for term reports and staff appraisal statements. "Quentin's thought processes are as lutulent as ever . . ."

**LYGOPHILIA** *n.* ❧ Love of darkness. A condition experienced in its most powerful form immediately after one has received the electricity bill.

**LYPOPHRENIA** *n.* ❧ A vague feeling of sadness, seemingly without cause. Mondayitis on Friday.

## ❧ M ❧

**MADERISE** *v.* ❧ To become flat in taste through absorbing too much oxygen while maturing (normally said of wines). "O.K.—who didn't screw down the top on the soda this time? It's maderised again."

**MALNOIA** *n.* ❧ A vague feeling of mental discomfort. At last—the word we all wanted, to describe the way we feel five minutes after waking up in the morning when we realize that we are about to recall yesterday's unresolved problems.

**MALVERSATION** *n.* ❧ Not, as might seem, an evil conversation, but improper or corrupt administration, especially when in a position of trust. Literally, bad behavior. "Now, ladies, this is the first confectionery committee meeting for the year, so let's get on with the agenda and leave the malversation till later."

MANDUCATE *v.* ❧ To chew or eat (with figurative over-tones—to "make a meal" out of something; to worry away at it). "I will say no more about your behavior last night, Daniel; it has already been the subject of more than adequate manducation by your mother . . ."

MANGELWURZEL *n.* ❧ Truly a word to revel in. Roll it round your tongue and belabor your fellow dinner guests with it at every opportunity—that is to say, whenever anything re-motely like a root vegetable is served. "How many of you know that the mangelwurzel, or more properly the mangold-wurzel, from mangold (beet) and wurzel (root) is a variety of beet cultivated for cattle food?" you might amiably enquire, looking up and down the table and holding aloft on fork's end a piece of sweet potato.

MARCID *a.* ❧ Exhausted, withered, wasted away—even de-cayed. Hence the Marcidity Allowance, which is available to civil servants with more than thirty years' substantive service.

MARITODESPOTISM *n.* ❧ Ruthless domination by a husband. Can such things be?

MATURATIVE *a.* ❧ Conducive to suppuration, as for in-stance to the formation of pus in an abscess. "Thanks for the socks, sis. It's what I really wanted for my birthday. I don't know—living with you sometimes seems so . . . maturative."

MATUTINAL *a.* ❧ Happening in the morning. A nicely ambiguous remark: "I often think of you as I'm having my matutinal." Matutinal what?, the hearer, having looked up the word itself, then wonders. And rightly so.

MEMBRANACEOUS *a.* ❧ Like a membrane; thin, translucent, papery. "I admire Arthur greatly for the way in which he has presented his case. His arguments, as always, are membranaceous . . ."

MENDACILOQUENT *a.* ❧ Speaking lies. Congressmen please note: if you say this quickly enough, on the floor of the House, when characterizing another Congressman (and God knows, in that environment you'll have plenty of occasions for so doing), the Speaker just might let you get away with it.

MENSEFUL *a.* ❧ Considerate, neat, and clean. A good one for the Personals: "Menseful lady wishes to meet ditto gent, view discreet exchange of courtesies."

MERACIOUS *a.* ❧ Unadulterated, full-strength, pure. "I'll say one thing about Bellamy—whatever other people say about him—you have to admit that all his sins are meracious ones."

METOPOSCOPY *n.* ❧ Judging character from the appearance of the face. A casual look in the bathroom mirror first thing in the morning will readily demonstrate the fallibility of this notion.

METROPHOBIA *n.* ❧ A morbid dread of poetry. It is believed that most cases can be traced back to a specific traumatic incident involving enforced exposure to the genre in concentrated form, e.g., a junior secondary school pupil being compelled to study a Shakespeare play or a Literary Editor being compelled to act as judge in a newspaper poetry competition.

Among noted metrophobes of recent times was the lexicographer Ambrose Bierce, who, in defining "incompossible," wrote that two things are incompossible when the world of being has scope enough for one of them but not enough for both, giving as his example Walt Whitman's poetry and God's mercy to man.

MICRONOETIC *a.* ❧ With minimal intellectual or cognitive content. "As Dean of the Faculty of Micronoetic Studies, I welcome all of you to this first meeting of the Academic Board. Now, are we all present? Educational Administration? Environmental Studies? Landscape Design? Catering Studies? Communication Studies? Social Administration? Community Studies? Multicultural Education? Ethnic Studies? Alternative Living Studies? Intercultural Studies? Park Administration? Recreation Planning? Good—now the first item on the agenda is our draft proposal for a new postdoctoral qualification in Bisexual Economics . . ."

MINIMIFIDIANISM *n.* ❧ Having almost no faith or belief. Condition of a commuter wondering if the train will arrive on time; of a householder wondering if the power blackout

*Metrophobia*

will end before dinnertime; or of a parent wondering if a teenager will place his dirty clothes in the laundry basket rather than on the floor under the bed.

MINNESINGER *n.* ❧ A thirteenth-century German writer/ singer of love lyrics. What the hell, let's be obvious with this one. Pronounce it mini-singer and use it when referring to *pyknic* (q.v.) tenors.

MINUEND *n.* ❧ The number from which another number (the "subtrahend") is taken away in a subtraction sum. Everyone knows about quotients, divisors, and so on, but not many people know about the minuend or the subtrahend, so use these terms remorselessly at every opportunity.

MISSION STATEMENT *n.* ❧ Not, as might be expected, an invoice received from a religious establishment, but the latest pretentious term from the world of New Management. It means "objectives," and seems to be largely replacing the previously popular "corporate plan." The comings and goings of the modish terminology of the New Managers, and the array of documentation that the terminology reflects, constitute a potential field of study for a doctoral thesis. A "Duty Statement," for example, is a job description worded in sufficiently elementary terms to enable a dimwitted candidate to apply for the job. "Selection Criteria" are descriptions of job qualifications worded in sufficiently elementary terms to enable a dimwitted selection panel member to select the wrong candidate. And so on.

MITHRIDATIZE *v.* ❧ To gradually make immune to a poison, by the consumption over a long period of increasing doses. From Mithridates, King of Pontus from 120 to 63 B.C., who is said to have so poison-proofed himself. "No, the spices won't worry me at all, Mrs. Krishnaswamy; after ten years of Maria's cooking, I'm completely mithridatized."

MOIETY *n.* ❧ Strictly speaking, this means "half" or at least "one of the parts of something that has been divided into two." In common parlance, however, it carries a suggestion of "fair share." (The common parlance referred to here is, of course, common parlance between two Supreme Court judges or two Professors of Linguistics; the term is not exactly an everyday one—but then that, after all, is why it's in this book, isn't it?) A cute little word. Nauseate your children even further, when carving the roast beef, slicing the birthday cake, etc., with an unctuous reference to your intention that each shall receive his or her moiety.

MOLENDINACEOUS *a.* ❧ Like a windmill. Mode of motion of two post-pubertal teenagers vying to be first to get downstairs, into the car, etc.

MONANDROUS *a.* ❧ Having one male mate at a time. Note that it is quite possible to be both monandrous and promiscuous, depending on the length of the time in question. "Is she promiscuous? Well, let's put it this way—it's a miracle she's monandrous at any one moment."

MONOGLOT *n.* ❧ Someone who is fluent in only one language. "I'm sorry, Janita, but I'll have to refrain from indulging in the jellied lambs' brains; I have this medical problem, you see—I'm a monoglot, and . . . "

MONSTRANCE *n.* ❧ The ornamental receptacle which is used to display the consecrated host to the congregation. Passing over the obvious opportunities for jokes about monsters and TV talk-show hosts, the responsible lexicographer can only point out that the derivation is the same as that of "demonstrate" (*monstrare*, to show) and invite the reader to develop his or her own whimsical use for the term. *Use*, please note, not *usage*; it is amazing how many people think the two words have the same meaning. The one means what it says—use—and the other means commonality of use. Unfortunately, the Big Is Better syndrome (see *pressurize*) is constantly pushing us to use the bigger of the available variants for any term, regardless of such considerations as nicety of meaning.

MONTICULOUS *a.* ❧ Having small projections. From "monticulus"—a small rise or elevation. A suitable and, ultimately, necessary alternative for "papuliferous" (pimply); your adolescent son is bound to find out sooner or later what you mean by that one.

*Monticulous*

MOROLOGY *n.* ❧ Nonsense; mere foolishness. "Allow me to introduce Professor Paramore, one of our leading morologists . . ."

MOROSIS *n.* ❧ Imbecility. "Why Belinda, the way you've done up the lounge room is just wonderful! It has this quality of . . . what the Portuguese call 'morosis,' I think. No one but you could have done it!"

MOUNSTER *n.* ❧ Old-fashioned form of "monster." "So good that young Lavinia is learning to ride a horse now. Look at them now; what a pair they make—mount and mounster."

MUMBLECRUST *n.* ❧ A toothless one; more figuratively, an old beggar. "And another thing—I'm fed up with having those mumblecrust relatives of yours around the place at all hours!"

MURCID *a.* ❧ Slothful, shirking work or duty. "Well, Grandpa, when I leave school I plan to do a university course while working part-time. In the medium to longer term, of course, I aspire to full-time murcidity."

MUSCID *a.* ❧ Pertaining to a housefly. "He's an irresponsible muckraker. His behavior is positively muscid."

MYCOID *a.* ❧ Like a fungus. Appearance of (*a*) unwashed socks found under teenager's bed after three weeks, or (*b*) unshaven face of teenage daughter's first boyfriend.

MYCOPHAGY *n.* ❧ The eating of fungi. "Mushroom soup, anyone? What, no mycophagists here?"

## ❧ N ❧

NAPALM *n.* ❧ Everyone now knows what napalm is, but did you know that the word is an abbreviation of "naphthenate palmitate"? Of course you didn't. Nor does your neighbor— the one with the three German Shepherds in his back yard. "Yes, I've noticed the dogs seem to be very restless after dark these days, Bill. Have you tried naphthenate palmitate? I hear it's very good for that sort of thing."

NASUTE *a.* ❧ Having an acute sense of smell. Do your best to arrange a blind date for such a person with a *tragomaschaliac* (q.v.).

NATATORIUM *n.* ❧ An indoor swimming pool. "If and when your brother surfaces from his seclusion in the bathroom and joins you at the TV, kindly inform him that the receptacle in which he has been so audibly disporting himself is a bath, not a natatorium."

NECESSITARIANISM *n.* ❧ A highfalutin word for determinism, i.e., the doctrine of inevitability of action resulting from a combination of hereditary and environmental influences. The opposite of the concept of free will. This puts the children of two necessitarianists in a peculiarly favorable position. "Yes, Mama, I know that I hit little Eric over the head with the vertical grill, and that he did lose consciousness for a moment, and, yes, that in falling he did break an ankle and also your Spode tureen. But Mama, as a necessitarianist you will appreciate that none of this is the result of an act of free will on my part. Indeed, it would seem that you and Papa, as my progenitors and the creators of my developmental environment, have a heavy responsibility to bear for what has happened . . ."

NECROMIMESIS *n.* ❧ A morbid mental state in which the sufferer believes himself to be dead. Not as common as the reverse condition, in which the sufferers believe themselves to be alive.

NECROMORPHOUS *a.* ❧ Feigning death to deter an aggressor. This would explain a lot about the behavior of counter staff in government departments.

NEOTENY *n.* ❧ An indefinite prolongation of the period of immaturity, with the retention of infantile or juvenile qualities into adulthood. Classic condition of the sports commentator, the lexicographer, and of course the schoolteacher.

NIDDERING *a.* ❧ Infamous, base, or cowardly. Or, one presumes, all three at once. A difficult combination to achieve, outside of the halls of Congress.

NIDIFUGOUS *a.* ❧ Leaving the nest while still young. "You're so lucky that Nicol and Mallory were nidifugous. If only I could say the same for Cyprian—especially now that he's started collecting punk ephemera."

NIPPERKIN *n.* ❧ An amount of liquor approximately equal to half a pint. "Who, me? Oh, I'll have . . . just a little nipperkin of scotch, thank you." Alternatively, you could ask for a nipperkin of nippitatum, which is an exceptionally good and strong ale.

NIPTER *n.* ❧ Ceremony of washing the feet on Maundy Thursday in the Eastern Orthodox church. Hang on . . . Maundy Thursday comes only *once a year!* On the face of it, this would seem to be a body blow to the cause of multiculturalism.

*Neotony*

NOCTIVAGANT *a.* ❧ Wandering by night. An undoctored cat; or the large huntsman spider that appears on a different ceiling each morning. "Sorry, Brett, I just don't know where Lisa is this evening; she's become rather noctivagant since she got her driver's license."

NOESIS *n.* ❧ The activity of the intellect in the process of cognition. "Jimmy showed more effort this term, and did well in sports, leadership, and honest endeavor, but his subject marks remained low. He should not be too discouraged by this, since he is doing as well as can be expected for someone without the advantage of the usual noesis."

NONFEASANCE *n.* ❧ Failure to perform some action which ought to have been performed. (Cf. *malfeasance*, official misconduct, and *misfeasance*, wrongful exercise of authority.) "You're looking just a trifle inimical tonight, oh my best beloved. Pray tell—have I committed malfeasance, misfeasance, or nonfeasance?"

NONPLUS *v.* ❧ To confuse or disconcert. A likeable word which ought to be used more often than it is. One of the more nonplussing things about it is how it came to mean what it does. It comes from the Latin *non plus*, i.e., "not more," and the derivation appears to be from medieval scholastic disputations when the out-argued disputant was said to have arrived at a non plus. Be that as it may, a nice way to nonplus your friends is to pronounce the term as "nun-ploss." It may prove possible to persuade the more gullible among them that this is the traditional eighteenth-century pronunciation. Of course, on the other hand this may serve merely to reinforce your already growing reputation as a boring old fart with a penchant for tedious whimsy.

NOSISM *n.* ❧ Collective egotism; group conceit. "Perhaps, Prime Minister, if your ministerial colleagues could group themselves more closely around you—that's right, shoulder to shoulder—we want everyone to be in the photo—perhaps with your arms on each other's shoulders—that's right—wonderful—we want to bring out the solidarity, the nosism, of the Cabinet as a whole . . ."

NOSTRIFICATE *v.* ❧ To accept as one's own. "Don't lean too far over the edge of the monkey pit, children; they are all too likely to nostrificate you."

NOTAPHILY *n.* ❧ The collecting of bank notes, as a hobby. (Curiously enough, the author himself pursues this hobby, specializing in present-day Australian dollar denominations. Readers who may be in a position to help him extend his collection are very welcome to do so; he knows you will appreciate that he pursues this interest for love, not money, and is unable to pay for any items that you may wish to volunteer.)

NOT A PROBLEM *phr.* ❧ This phrase, which is currently much in vogue with car salespeople, insurance agents, and their ilk, means more or less "that's a real problem you've thrown at me, man, and I'll need time to come up with some ploy to gloss over the difficulty."

NUCIVOROUS *a.* ❧ Nut-eating. "I see that Andrew's idea of putting out some hors d'oeuvres for our guests is to set out a dozen bowls full of assorted nuts. Not surprising, I suppose, given that he's surrounded at the office by people who are either parrots or apes." (Raising her voice:) "What time are the nucivores arriving, darling?"

NUGACITY *n.* ❧ Triviality, futility. "Why not ask Boris and Deirdre? Add a touch of nugacity to the evening?"

NULLIBIST *n.* ❧ One who denies the existence of the soul in space. "Now that we're in orbit, Teresa, you will appreciate that as a confirmed nullibist I have no sense of moral obligation, and will not have any until reentry in three days' time. So how's about a little you-know-what, cookie, or would you rather I farted in your oxygen supply?"

NUMINOUS *a.* ❧ Divine. Like a deity in human form. You may wish to so characterize your beloved—but in that event first make sure that she knows what it means. Best to buy her a copy of this book right now, in fact.

NUNCHEON *n.* ❧ A noon drink. "I'll just leave the accounts till this afternoon if you don't mind, Miles; I find that I'm running late for a nuncheon appointment."

NUTATION *n.* ❧ The act of nodding; more specifically, habitual or constant nodding of the head. "Hickmott would be a very sound choice to head your Department, Minister—always gives full value—state-of-the-art nutation, day in, day out."

NUTRICISM *n.* ❧ A form of symbiosis in which one of the two organisms involved is nourished or protected by the other without making any reciprocal contribution. Parenthood, presumably.

NYCTERENT *a.* ❧ One who hunts by night. A dog looking for a loose-lidded garbage can to push over and disembowel spectacularly. A garbage can owner looking for a nycterent dog. A lovesick teenager looking for another lovesick teenager.

NYCTITROPIC *a.* ❧ Turning in a certain direction at night. "Brendan's nyctitropic. Put him outside at night and he turns in the direction of the nearest bar."

NYCTOPHONIAC *a.* ❧ Able to give voice only at night. The neighborhood dog that remains miraculously silent all day but becomes remarkably voluble after midnight.

## ❧ O ❧

OBAMBULATE *v.* ❧ To wander or walk about in an aimless fashion. The motion of a male spouse in a Sunday morning flea market or a female spouse in a department store. "For heaven's sake, where's your father got to now? He's gone obambulating again, just when it's time to go home."

OBLIQUITY *n.* ❧ Deviation. "Tried any new obliquities this week, Simon?"

OBLONGITUDE *n.* ❧ Believe it or not, the state of being oblong. The "g" is pronounced "j." "You've done it at last, Mrs. Mummery; a cake with real oblongitude!"

OBSOLAGNIUM *n.* ❧ Waning sexual desire due to age. A mythical condition invented by the young folk, who, already chafing from the knowledge that their elders have more power, more experience, more savoir faire, more knowledge, and more money than they do, feel obliged to postulate some equalizing disadvantage. Bad luck, kiddies. Not only do we get more of it than you, but for us it's safer as well.

OBTUND *v.* ❧ To blunt, dull, or deaden. "And now, dear colleagues, as the evening comes to a close, to thoroughly obtund all our conviviality, all the exchanges of ideas and enthusiasms that we have shared tonight, here is our final speaker, the Chairman of the Board, Sir Maurice himself!"

OCCULTATION *n.* ❧ Being hidden from view, or lost to notice. An astronomical term, referring specifically to the extinction of a heavenly body's light by the intervention of another. Such as Miss U.S.A. inadvertently or otherwise stepping between Miss Sweden and the camera.

OCULOGYRIC *a.* ❧ Eye-rolling. "Attention all male children in this household above the age of ten! Your mother is enquiring about the origin of certain muddy footprints found on the living room carpet. Report to your mother at once, and be warned—whilst total frenzy has not yet occurred, the oculogyric phase has already commenced!"

OLIGOTROPHIA *n.* ❧ Lack of nourishment. Alleged condition of the teenage human male even after regularly consuming one family-sized pizza, six slices of buttered toast, one giant-size packet of potato chips, and one quart of chocolate milk, in between and in addition to any two normal meals.

OLLA-PODRIDA *n.* ❧ A Spanish mixed hash of meat and vegetables, or indeed any incongruous combination of leftovers from the bottom shelf of the fridge. Literally, "rotten pot." A suggested addition to your *Who's Who* entry, under Hobbies: "Playing the harpsichord; collecting early Oriental porcelain; and making olla-podrida fritters at dead of night."

OMBROPHILOUS *a.* ❧ Capable of withstanding heavy and continuous rain. For example, tropical vegetation. The correct epithet for a preschool child who has been got up for the day by his mother in gumboots, a knee-length raincoat, a rain-hat, and a miniature umbrella.

ONEIRODYNIA *n.* ❧ Nightmare. "If it turns out to be a girl, have you thought of giving her one of those lovely, mellifluous, ancient Greek names? Lydia, say, or Persephone? Or perhaps . . . Oneirodynia?"

ONERABLE *a.* ✤ Nothing to do with "honorable." Instead, a variant form of "onerous," i.e., burdensome or troublesome. "I see you've invited the Colonel. He's an onerable old stick, isn't he?"

ONOMASTICON *n.* ✤ An ordered list of names. "Mom, Hugo's in his bedroom, using the phone book as his personal onomasticon again! Can't you do anything about it? It's just disgusting!"

ONYCHOPHAGY *n.* ✤ Nail-biting. "With those remarks I conclude my address tonight on the issues facing you at this election. In a few minutes my opponent will take the floor— but before he does, I want him to know something. I have proof positive, in the form of this video recording, which I have in my hand—a video shot with a concealed camera—that this man, who puts himself forward as a suitable candidate to represent you in the halls of Congress—this man, this very same man, regularly indulges in onychophagy. I have arranged for the video to be shown on the large screen behind me, at the conclusion of his speech. That is all. Over to you, now, Mr. Hilary. Don't forget your lines."

OPHELIMITY *n.* ✤ The primary meaning is "the ability to please sexually"; but there is also a secondary meaning, "the ability to please generally"—a useful ambiguity which should allow you to gain a certain degree of quiet enjoyment from the use of the term.

OPISTHOPOREIA *n.* ✤ Involuntary walking backward. Apart from walking up the down escalator, it is hard (though amusing) to conceive a case of this. How would the sufferer ever get to work in the morning? And, much more worrying from the sufferer's point of view, how would he get home?

OPOPANAX *n.* ❧ Aromatic gum resin used in perfumery. "Lucille has opopanaxed the third floor again—she's been up there only five minutes, and eleven people have already come down with hay fever."

OPSABLEPSIA *n.* ❧ Not looking into another's eyes. In some cultures a sign of disrespect or evasion; in others a sign of respect and deference. Make what you will of this.

OPSIGAMY *n.* ❧ Marriage late in life. All things considered, probably a better fate than *opsiproligery*, which is the ability to have children late in life.

ORARIAN *n.* ❧ Dweller by the seashore. Goes well with *otiant* (q.v.).

ORCHIDECTOMY *n.* ❧ Not, as you might think, an operation to cut out your orchids, but an operation to cut out something even more important. Orchidectomy is castration. Perhaps a florist, in dealing with unpleasant customers: "A thousand apologies, monsieur et madame, that we have no Yugoslavian peonies; perhaps by way of compensation I could offer madame, with the compliments of the firm, this petite corsage, and monsieur, perhaps" (here waving the pruning shears), "a leetle orchidectomy?"

ORGULOUS *a.* ❧ Proud, haughty, showy. "The decorations are marvelous, Cynthia dear! How perfectly orgulous of you!"

ORTHOBIOSIS *n.* ❧ A hygienic and moral life style. "Well, your qualifications and career history seem very relevant. How is your health? No arthritis, no orthobiosis, I hope?"

ORTHOPTEROUS *a.* ❧ To do with insects; insectlike. "Now look here, you orthopterous creep . . ."

*Orthopterous*

ORTHOSIS *n.* ❧ The correction of a neurotic state. "Poor dear! He/she has tried chiropracty, homeopathy, naturopathy, *and* iridology—and I remember telling him/her in the first place that all he/she needed was a little orthosis."

ORTHOSTATIC *a.* ❧ Pertaining to standing upright. "What a dilemma for Nicholas! Orthostatic coma! Still, I suppose it must be some consolation to Marge to know that she's married to a medical miracle . . ."

OSOPHAGIST *n.* ❧ A fastidious eater. One who picks and chooses. Adolescent children are by nature and inclination osophagic, and moreover their respective osophagies are rarely coincident. Thus the need, in a two-adolescent family, for two different brands of sauce, two different methods of cleaning the silverware, two different ways of cooking the french fries, etc., etc. This is known as multiple osophagy, and increases exponentially with the number of children involved.

OTIANT *a.* ❧ Idle or resting. The author's dearest wish is to be an otiant *orarian* (q.v.).

OVIFORM or OVINE *a.* ❧ Like a sheep. The movement or behavior pattern of a one-day golfing crowd.

OZOSTOMIA *n.* ❧ Evil-smelling breath. Or so my source defines it. Not bad, you will note, not sour; but *evil*. How does breath smell evil? Is this the origin of the famous royal motto "Evil be to him who evil stinks"?

Or have I got that wrong?

## ❧ P ❧

PABULUM *n.* ❧ The means of nutrient for animals or plants. Food as a basic fuel, as distinct from any aesthetic or appetizing qualities that it may have. "Ah, Lady Mountjoy, as always—you offer your fortunate guests pabulum—pure pabulum!"

PAIZOGONY *n.* ❧ Love play. "I know this great little Italian take-out restaurant. Let's go down there first and then go to the drive-in and have some paizogony in the car."

PANDAEMONIUM *n.* ❧ Commonly spelled "pandemonium" and taken to mean a great noise and disorder; but actually the capital city of Hell in Milton's *Paradise Lost*. In the full knowledge of its original meaning, and *always* giving full value to the central diphthong when pronouncing it, you might so refer to the rumpus room, your youngest child's bedroom, etc.

PANPSYCHIST *n.* ❧ One who believes that everything, whether animal, vegetable, or mineral, has a soul. Perhaps today's paradigmatic panpsychist is the young lady who gives her hatchback a Christian name and speaks affectionately of it by that name. On the other hand, there are also the people who play music to flowers. And the gamblers who harangue their dice. And the homemakers who stand at their front doors, shouting "Grow, you bastard, grow!" at a newly seeded lawn. But perhaps the ultimate in panpsychism is a case known to the author—a person whose idealism was so unstinting that he once attempted to have a conversation with a certified public accountant.

PANTOPHAGY *n.* ❧ Omnivorousness, i.e., eating anything and everything. "Sorry to have to say this about my brother, but I should let you know about him if you're really thinking of inviting him into your house. The fact is he's . . . er, well . . . I'm ashamed to say this but I suppose I have to . . . he's pantophagous."

PANTOPHOBIA *n.* ❧ The morbid fear of everything. There had to be a name for it. Fortunately it hits most of us for only a few minutes at a time.

PARACME *n.* ❧ The stage after one's peak, when decline and senescence set in. "What an idea, Professor! You are indeed at the paracme of your powers!"

PARADIASTOLE *n.* ❧ A euphemistic half-truth. "Gosh, dear, you look fabulous in your new dress—no really, I mean it—paradiastoles fail me."

PAROREXIA *n.* ❧ A perverted appetite, or craving for strange foods. Supposedly the condition of gravid females, but more classically the condition of *(a)* the adolescent human male ("Don't be like that, Dad—haven't you ever seen a two-minute noodles and tomato sauce toasted sandwich before?") and *(b)* the gastronomic parvenu ("I've found this absolutely *wonderful* little Provençal restaurant—my dear, their marinated hedgehog in quince sauce with just a *little* more garlic than usual—delicious!")

*Parorexia*

PECULATE *v.* ❧ To pilfer or embezzle. Etymologically quite distinct from "speculate," but many do both while under the impression that they are doing only the one or the other.

PEDUNCLE *n.* ❧ A stalklike appendage in a biological organism. Chambers defines it, mysteriously, as "the stalk by which a sedentary animal is attached." Attached to what? And what is a sedentary animal? A civil servant? And if so, what is the civil servant attached to? Best perhaps to leave these questions to older and wiser heads—which themselves have their own peduncles, incidentally, since a peduncle is also "a tract of white fibres in the brain." Be that as it may, this is a word that cries out for greater use in conversation. Talk to your friends about your peduncle. Ask them about theirs. Do your bit to increase appendage-consciousness in the community at large.

PERISTALSIS *n.* ❧ The contractions of the alimentary canal in the process of digestion. "How fitting," you might say to the avant-garde composer after the premiere of his latest threnody for guitar, cowbells, and synthesizer; "how fitting were those peristaltic rhythms for that last, for want of a better word, movement."

PERNICKETY *a.* ❧ Finical (always to be preferred to the more commonly used "finicky"), fussy, fastidious. Not many people know that this word was invented by A. A. Milne when searching for a rhyme for "rickety" in a humorous poem about an impoverished king. (You don't get this sort of information in the American Heritage Dictionary.)

PHANEROMANIA *n.* ❧ A compulsion to pick at a skin growth or imperfection. Is there *anyone* who doesn't suffer from this?

PHORONOMICS *n.* ❧ Kinematics, i.e., the science of motion. The cinema is called the cinema today because it began as the cinematograph, which was originally called the kinematograph, i.e., that which transcribes motions. This gives you the choice of annoying your film buff friends by speaking of the cinema as the "kinema" or baffling them by referring to it as the "phoronomograph."

PICAROON *n.* ❧ A vagabond. Someone who lives by his wits. A rogue. The suggestion, furthermore, is of a *lovable* rogue. A professional talk-show guest, a tax evader, a financial advisor, a politician's press secretary, et al.

PICAYUNE *a.* ❧ Trifling, paltry. Too small or insignificant to be worth consideration. A picayune was an early-nineteenth-century American coin of small value. "Father, don't you think that my weekly allowance has become somewhat picayune with the passage of time?"

PINUS RADIATA *n.* ❧ A common type of pine tree, otherwise known as radiata pine; with shrubs, trees, etc. the so-called "scientific" name is always to be preferred, pronounced of course as Latin, not Anglicized. Thus "i" is pronounced "ee," not "eye."

PIS ALLER *n.* ❧ A makeshift. Something that will do for lack of anything better. From *pis*, worse, and *aller*, to go. No relation to a *pismire*, which is simply an ant, and which in turn has no relation to *piss-ant*, a term mistakenly used by the ignorant as one of contempt when in fact it is a variant of *puissant*, i.e., powerful.

PISIFORM *a.* ❧ Pea-shaped. 'Nuff said?

PLEIONOSIS *n.* ❧ The exaggeration of one's own importance. The only disorder universal to humankind.

PLENILOQUENCE *n.* ❧ Literally, a plenitude of talking. Excessive loquacity. There are two species of the genus, entitled the Senate and the House of Representatives.

PNIGEROPHOBIA *n.* ❧ A morbid dread of being smothered. The only real disincentive to union with a *viscerotonic* (q.v.).

POGONOPHOBIA *n.* ❧ A morbid dread of beards. As many *whilom* (q.v.) bearded ones can attest, the severity of this complaint is as nothing compared with the severity of its opposite number—the morbid dread by family members of a face from which a beard has just been removed.

POLIOSIS *n.* ❧ Premature greying of the hair. A puzzling concept—after all, what greying of the hair is *not* premature?

POLYPHAGIA *n.* ❧ Excessive eating. "Ah, yuletide! Blessed season of joy! The Christmas tree, the decorations, the gifts, the carols, the sleigh bells, the *eructations* (q.v.), the polyphagia . . . "

PONOPHOBIA *n.* ❧ A morbid dread of work. Think about it. A civil servant could get a whole lifetime's sick leave out of this.

PORIOMANIA *n.* ❧ Wanderlust. A disease of cats, teenagers, and elderly ladies.

PRELIBATION *n.* ❧ Foretaste. The drink you have before you have a drink. And why not? Then there's postlibation too, of course. "I can only repeat, Felicity—I have not had a single drink—merely a series of prelibations and of course the necessary postlibations."

PRESCIND *v.* ❧ To cut off prematurely or abruptly. "With Colonel Ferrier's concurrence, we will prescind his contribution to tonight's discussion. That O.K., Colonel?"

PRESSURIZE *v.* ❧ Press. In future centuries, philologists will look back at the twentieth and characterize it as, verbally, the Age of Aggrandizement. What personal or societal traits this reflects is a matter for speculation by others; but certain it is that our natural tendency seems to be to create a noun out of a verb, and then convert the new noun into another and longer verb—a process which can be extended indefinitely. In the present case, the next step will probably be to replace "pressure" with "pressurization," which will in turn come to be used itself as a verb. And so on. The Big Is Better syndrome has us by the throat.

PRETERMIT *v.* ❧ To pass over something, ignoring it or leaving it unattended to for the time being. "Well, as Chairman I have to say that if Dr. Applehead feels so strongly about this agenda item, I think the rest of us would like to give him the opportunity, here and now, to pretermit it. Do you agree, Doctor?"

PRINK *v.* ❧ To deck out or smarten generally. "Prink yourself up, Fotherway, or it'll be the worse for you."

PROCTALGIA *n.* ❧ Pain in the backside. ("Rectalgia" means the same.) "And this is our Corporate Resources Management Officer . . . I'm sorry, her name has just slipped my mind for the moment, but she's known to all of us, with the greatest possible affection, as Proctalgia."

PROCUMBENT *a.* ❧ Lying or kneeling facedown; prostrate. "And another thing—I'd appreciate a little procumbency from you in future, Whittington."

PROLICIDE *a.* ❧ The killing of offspring. "Oh . . . were you thinking of bringing the kids too, Carol? . . . Oh well, that's all right . . . No don't worry, *please* bring them . . . it's really all right . . . I'm sure I can arrange a little prolicide for them . . ."

PROLUSION *n.* ❧ A preliminary performance or attempt. A trial run or abbreviated effort, in preparation for the real thing. Thus a *matutinal* (q.v.) upbraiding by a spouse may be a mere prolusion for the full event at eventide.

PROPAEDEUTIC *n.* ❧ Preliminary study. "The doctor said I'm allergic to propaedeutic, Mum, and I'm not to have any at night."

PROSOPOGRAPHY *n.* ❧ The total description of a person—his or her appearance, personality, social status, family connections, qualifications, employment history, etc. The ultimate résumé. "Candidates are asked to submit three copies of their prosopograph."

PROSOPOPOEIA *n.* ❧ A rhetorical introduction of an imagined speaker or a personification of some abstraction or inanimate object. "If these stones could speak . . ." "As I stand here, tonight, I hear the voice of my late wife—pray God this is prosopopoeia and not one of my delusional states . . ."

PROTERVITY *n.* ✣ Petulance. "Ah, Belinda, there is something so . . . so *young* about you . . . a kind of . . . how can I describe it . . . a kind of childlike . . . protervity . . . "

PROTOGENAL *a.* ✣ Pertaining to primitive creatures. "Come on, we want your kids in the photo too, Cousin Sal! Line them up in front—that'll make the picture more protogenal!"

PSEPHOLOGY *n.* ✣ The alleged science of fortune-telling, the fortunes in this case being those of the mega-cephalic but micro-minded posturers who periodically parade themselves before us, seeking political power, position, postage allowance, and pension. In short, psephology is the study of voting patterns at elections. Don't think too harshly of the psephologists. It's dirty work, but someone has to do it.

PYKNIC *a.* ✣ (Pronounced the same as "picnic.") Short and squat in build, with small hands and feet, short limbs and neck, a round face, and a domed abdomen. "I see he has the true pyknic build," you remark to Althea about her new and proudly displayed baby; "strange—I thought that was always inherited. Heavens, I don't suppose . . . ?"

✣ Q ✣

QHYTHSONTYD *n.* ✣ Whether it's for fitting something into a seemingly impossible situation on a crowded Scrabble board, or nonplussing the smart alecks in a spelling competition, or meeting the challenge to produce yet another "Q" word without a "u" after the "Q," or discountenancing someone who claims she can pronounce *anything* . . . The meaning hardly matters, does it? But just to prove it isn't made up: qhythsontyd is an obsolete form of the rather better-known "whitsuntide," i.e., Whit Sunday, the seventh Sunday after Easter.

QUAB *n.* ❧ A very small fish; or something immature or unfinished. The latter meaning would appear to be a metaphorical derivative of the former. "So they've made little Kenny head of the Department? Not surprised. He's a quab, but his *nutation* (q.v.) skills are awesome."

QUADDLE *v.* ❧ To grumble. To be a quaddler seems somehow to sound more amiable than to be a grumbler. "He's a loveable old quaddler."

QUAESTUARY *n.* ❧ Someone whose first and foremost objective is profit. A teenage son who will work in the garden only if paid to do so.

QUAG *n.* ❧ A boggy place, especially one that quakes underfoot. "Simon! Come here this minute and clean up your room! Do you realize that the area around and under your bed is pure quag?"

QUAGGLE *n.* ❧ A quivering, as of jelly. "And our special prize for the waltz competition tonight goes to Mrs. Broadbeem, for her unique Quaggle Effect."

QUAINTISE *n.* ❧ A cunning little ploy or stratagem. One for the weekly executive group meeting: "Well, Mr. Wetherby, what little quaintise do you have in store for us this morning, under Other Business?

QUIDNUNC *n.* ❧ A newsmonger or gossip. One is never just a quidnunc; one is an *inveterate* quidnunc. Not to be confused with "quincunx," an arrangement of five things in such a way that four of them are the points of a square and the fifth is in the center of the square.

QUILLET *n.* ❧ A subtlety in argument. "And what's more, in all the many speeches that Quentin has made over the years in the Senate, there has never been so much as a hint of personal vilification or the use of quillets to aid his case."

QUINK *n.* ❧ The common brant (a kind of goose). Conversation Stopper No. 331: "Did you know that the quink was the common brant?"

QUINT *n.* ❧ A pipe organ stop, which sounds at the interval of a fifth above the key depressed. In case you think that this is an odd name for an organ stop, here are some others: Amorosa (a hybrid flute stop); Bearded Gamba (a string stop "of keen and cutting quality"); Chimney Flute (a half-covered flute); Clarabella (an open wood flute); Copula (I'm not saying what that one does); Corno Di Bassetto (basset horn—Bernard Shaw's *nom de plume* as a music critic); Gravissima (I had thought this meant a very pregnant lady, but according to my source it gives the organist "an impressive bottom for his combinations"); Gross Quint (gross quint); Heckelphone (unaccountably, there appears to be no Jeckelphone); Krummhorn ("mournful and sedate"); Ludwigtone (sounding like Ludwig); Stentorphone (you've guessed it—very loud); Suave Flute (suave flute—would not be seen dead with Gross Quint); Tibia Dura (shinbone—no, only joking); Tuba d'Amour (love tube—keep well away from Copula); Viol Quint (vile quint—often seen with Gross Quint); and Zink ("pungent, nasal"). I have made up none of these names, many of which, incidentally, have an obvious potentiality of application to the world of human types. All of us know a few Zinks, for example.

QUONDAM *a.* ❧ Whilom (q.v.). Enough said?

## ❧ R ❧

RADDLED *a.* ❧ Most of us have heard this expression used of someone who is getting on in years and is in a confused state—meaning more or less "old and silly." But the actual meaning is, to quote Chambers, "aged and worsened by debauchery." From "reddle"—red ocher, or coarse rouge, referring to the rouging of elderly roués' cheeks, particularly in the eighteenth century. Be not too unkind in the way that you use this knowledge.

REBOANT *a.* ❧ Reverberating very loudly. "Remember, children, this is a chapel of remembrance; when we're inside would you all please lower your voice to about reboant level."

RECALESCENT *a.* ❧ Glowing with heat again, temporarily, at a certain stage of the process of cooling down from white heat. A fitting epithet for an elderly acquaintance who is making a fool of himself with a *poppet* or a *frippet* (q.v.), and having the time of his life in the process.

REDHIBITION *n.* ❧ The nullification of a sale because of a defect in the article sold. Something to say when the priest asks whether you will take this person to be your lawful wedded spouse: "Are there redhibition rights on this contract? Only joking!"

REFOCILLATION *n.* ❧ Total refreshment; revival or revitalization. You stagger into the bar, collapse onto the stool immediately facing the *bathycolpian* (q.v.) barmaid, and gasp: "Refocillate me!" Whether she understands or misunderstands you, there is at least some chance that you will achieve refocillation.

REGELATION *n.* ❧ Freezing together again, after having melted apart (as ice may, when it is subject to changing levels of pressure). "So Jonquil and Bruce are together again, eh? Five years after their divorce—fancy that! Are they going to have a regelation ceremony?"

REMONTADO *n.* ❧ Someone who has fled to the mountains and renounced civilization. A ski instructor.

REMPLISSAGE *n.* ❧ Padding, i.e., needless filling, in literature. From the French, naturally. Not possible in a highly structured work of the present nature, but rampant in lesser forms such as the novel (which, as everyone knows, is merely a story with remplissage), the TV weather report, and the lawyer's bill of accounts.

RENIFORM *a.* ❧ Kidney-shaped. "Kind of you to ask after me, Maurice. As it happens, I've just had some rather important news. Had a chat with my doctor, and it seems I have reniform kidneys."

RENITENCY *n.* ❧ Reluctance or resistance. "Don't worry, Dad; the idea of a weekly work assignment in return for my allowance is one that I can handle with complete renitency."

REPTATION *n.* ❧ The motion of two plane figures (flat surfaces, you ignoramuses) when they are slid around against each other. A mathematical term which derives from "reptile," its alternative meaning being "creeping like a reptile." Hence the sense can reasonably be extended to characterize the locomotion of the figuratively reptilian. "Our courses for encyclopaedia salespersons, insurance agents, investment advisers, and senior banking executives include basic accounting, business principles, communication, and reptation skills . . ."

RESUPINATE *a.* ❧ Upside down as a result of twisting. "So sad about Bannister. Been in politics only seven years and already suffering irreversible resupination."

RETROBULBAR *a.* ❧ Behind the eyeball. Since this is (more or less) where the brain is, I suppose you could refer to an ideological adversary as being "disadvantaged by a retrobulbar vacancy."

RETRUSION *n.* ❧ A displacement of the teeth toward the back of the mouth. "If the Honorable Senator is so unhappy about my remarks, I would invite him to meet me afterward in the corridor, where I will be happy to give him a complete retrusion."

RHADAMANTHINE *a.* ❧ Uncompromisingly just and completely incorruptible. From Rhadamanthus, a mythical Greek judge, and therefore an epithet normally reserved for persons in judicial positions. It is said, however, that there was once a rhadamanthine politician.

RHATHYMIA *n.* ❧ Carefree, indifferent, or light-hearted behavior. "Now boys, this is a solemn ceremony; when the school chaplain gives his address, let's have some genuine rhathymia."

RHONCHISONANT *a.* ❧ This means snoring or snorting, but will sound a lot better than those terms when you put your self-description in the Personals.

RHYTIDECTOMY *n.* ❧ A surgical operation in which the skin of the face is smoothed out and wrinkles removed. Commonly called a face-lift. "Fancy meeting you after all these years, Meredith! I nearly didn't recognize you. And how wise of you not to have had a rhytidectomy, in spite of everything!"

*Rhytidectomy*

RHYTISCOPIA *n.* ❧ A neurotic preoccupation with facial wrinkles. "Elissa, how you've changed! Oh, I do hope you're not troubled by rhytiscopia!"

RIGIDULOUS *a.* ❧ Somewhat rigid; a little stiff. A tricky word, looking as it does so much like a misprint for "ridiculous." Not easy to say, either—try it, and you'll see what I mean.

RINDERPEST *n.* ❧ A malignant and contagious disease of cattle. "I'd like to tell that child exactly what I think of him, but I can't decide whether he's got the rinderpest or whether he *is* the rinderpest."

RISORGIMENTO *n.* ❧ A revival of artistic, liberal, or national spirit. However, in the hurly-burly of an Italian restaurant, it is almost always possible to convince at least one of your table companions that it is in fact a vegetarian pasta dish, and induce her to order it from a passing waiter.

ROINOUS *a.* ❧ Mean, nasty, and contemptible. "I'll let Adrian speak for himself, and we'll all see just how roinous he can be."

ROUNCEVAL *n.* ❧ Three quite different meanings for this one: a giant; a marrowfat pea; and a virago. Nice to be able to characterize something or someone with a term that is not just ambiguous but doubly so. "A new book, eh, Lorraine? What a thoroughgoing rounceval you are!"

RUDERAL *n.* ❧ Thriving in rubbish or waste. A term from the world of plant life that has obvious potential for application to the animal world. "She's had a truly ruderal career, you know—she's done well, first as secretary to a backbencher, then on the Minister's research staff, and now as executive assistant for the party leader."

RUPTUARY *n.* ❧ A commoner or plebeian. One of the few words that rhymes with "voluptuary." "So glad you're in the insurance game now, Ernestine; it always seemed to me that you were suited for ruptuarial work."

RUTILANT *a.* ❧ Glittering or glowing with reddish light. Your Uncle Arbuthnot's nose after a hard day's social intercourse.

# ✤ S ✤

**SACKBUT** *n.* ✤ A medieval instrument, not unlike a trombone. The term is derived from an old French word for a hook used to pull a man off a horse. Make what you will of this.

**SAXICOLOUS** *a.* ✤ Living or growing among rocks. A geology student.

**SCOPODROMIC** *a.* ✤ Pertaining to the motion of a guided missile homing in on its target. "You're not just putting the gingerbread men in the cookie jar, surely? Don't forget you-know-who's scopodromic qualities. What about the wall safe?"

**SCOPOPHOBIA** *n.* ✤ A morbid fear of being seen. "Scotophobia" is a morbid fear of darkness. How appalling to suffer from both simultaneously! Think about it.

**SCORDATURA** *n.* ✤ An unusual tuning of a stringed instrument, intended to achieve a special effect. Convenient for use as a polite euphemism when invited to comment on the violin playing of your host's ten-year-old. "Hmm, interesting scordatura there—very interesting!"

**SCRIVENER** *n.* ✤ A copyist of documents. One employed solely to copy out legal or financial documents by hand. A nineteenth-century occupation made famous forever by Melville's classic story *Bartleby the Scrivener,* in which the inoffensive Bartleby refuses any work other than copying, and quietly remains at his place of work while the work itself moves on, leaving him with nothing to do but die. An allegory for the age of micro-computers and multi-skilling. Honor Bartleby by refusing to use the term Carpal Tunnel Syndrome and insisting on referring to your condition instead as "scrivener's palsy"— the old-fashioned term for writer's cramp.

SCUMBLE *v.* ❧ To lay a thin coat of opaque or nearly opaque color over a painted area with an almost dry brush, to soften the color or line of a picture. An endearingly unsophisticated word for such a sophisticated process. "I'm sorry, he can't come to the phone; he's busy scumbling."

SENESCHAL *n.* ❧ The steward or majordomo of a medieval mansion or cathedral. The school janitor, perhaps?

SIALOGOGUE *n.* ❧ Something that stimulates the flow of saliva. "Ah, Rachel, a quiet little dinner party like this, with just the two of us . . . and you the perfect sialogogue."

SICARIAN *n.* ❧ A murderer. More specifically, an assassin. "You'll find 3B an interesting class this year, Carruthers. Very multicultural. There are some Lebanese, a couple of Croatians and Serbs . . . watch out for the two Irish kids—they're from opposite sides in Ulster . . . there's a Calabrian and a Sicilian . . . as for the others, they're mainly sicarians, I think."

SIDERATION *n.* ❧ The use of green manure. "Sorry to see you're having trouble with your complexion again, Candace. Collagen not working, eh? Have you thought of trying a little sideration?"

SILLABUB *n.* ❧ A dessert made mostly out of cream. A pleasing, eighteenth-centuryish term for the jar of creamed rice that you are obliged to open for your unexpected dinner guest. Metaphorically, sillabub is inane, inconsequential, or frothy speech.

SITOPHOBIA *n.* ♣ Morbid fear of eating. Not common in its general form, but often encountered in its various specific forms, e.g., fear of eating your mother-in-law's garlic broccoli, fear of eating your small daughter's rock cakes, etc.

SKULDUGGERY *n.* ♣ Dirty work. Common words sometimes have uncommon alternative forms and indeed meanings. These the Superior Person always prefers. Thus "skulduddery" and its eighteenth-century sense of "unchastity" will enable you to add a little life to this somewhat tired pejorative.

SLUBBER *v.* ♣ To smear or dirty something, or to wallow in something. Three-year-olds and politicians are good slubberers.

SMATCHET *n.* ♣ A small, nasty person, or a nasty child. "Why, Carol—you've brought the twins! Gosh, when I see them together—smatchet and smatchet—I think I'm seeing double!"

SMEW *n.* ♣ A small species of merganser. Last-ditch-conversational-ploys-when-all-else-has-failed, No. 317: "Did you know that the smew is a small species of merganser?"

SNOOD *n.* ♣ A band for the hair, formerly regarded in Scotland as a badge of virginity. Not a bad term, perhaps, for the headbands now modishly worn by macho sportsmen—most of whom are probably virgins anyway, if what I hear about steroids is correct.

SOFFIT *n.* ♣ An architectural term meaning "the underside of an arch." The possibilites for using the term (albeit with a little poetic license) in relation to the human body are too obvious—indeed, some may think, too indelicate— to be spelled out here.

SOLATION *n.* ❧ The liquefaction of a gel. "Come in out of the rain, for heaven's sake, before solation sets in with that hairdo of yours."

SOPHOMANIA *n.* ❧ A delusional state in which the sufferer believes that he or she is a person of exceptional intelligence. Standard therapeutic procedure is for the sufferer to write a letter to the editor of a newspaper on a subject of current controversy; this invariably induces large numbers of other sufferers to write to the editor, telling the original sufferer what a fool he is. If therapy fails and the sufferer succumbs, he or she may be doomed to end his or her days as an economist.

SOTERIAL *a.* ❧ Pertaining to salvation. Thus *soteriology* is the doctrine of salvation. "Harrison, you are the living refutation of soteriology."

SPALLATION *n.* ❧ The splitting of the nucleus of an atom into many fragments as a result of high-energy bombardment. "Hey, Bob, guess what—Mom's got Dad in the kitchen and she's giving him one of her lectures. He's reached the hands-over-the-ears-and-face-turning-red stage. I'd say spallation must be imminent. Let's go and watch."

STAUROPHOBIA *n.* ❧ Pathological aversion to the cross or crucifix. Yes, this is it—the actual technical name for the condition which you have seen represented on the silver screen by countless actors lumbered with the task of portraying Dracula or other vampires and assorted evil spirits. This gives you the opportunity for much innocent byplay when you realize that the breast of your beloved is adorned by a pendant gold cross. With the standard *molendinaceous* (q.v.) arm wavings, baffled snarlings, and expressions of abject terror, you could recoil before the said cross, later shyly admitting to your staurophobia and stressing its standing as a recognized medical condition. And then, the cross removed, demonstrating your affection and gratitude with a little love-bite on the neck . . .

STEGOPHILIST *n.* ❧ One whose hobby is climbing the outside of tall buildings. "So you're suffering from fear of heights now, dearest? Hmm . . . have you thought of trying a little stegophily?"

STRAMINEOUS *a.* ❧ Strawlike, valueless. "Such a pleasure to debate an issue with you, Herr Doktor. I always find your arguments so . . . stramineous."

STRUTHIOUS *a.* ❧ Like an ostrich. A term of contempt for middle management.

SUANT *a.* ❧ Smooth, even, placid, agreeable, demure. If there is anyone out there who is both suant *and menseful* (q.v.), don't step under a bus—you are probably the last of your kind.

SUCCUSSION *n.* ❧ Shaking. It is not widely known that Jerry Lee Lewis' *magnum opus* "Whole lotta shakin' goin' on" was in fact originally written as "Whole lotta succussion goin' on" but subsequently changed when the League of American Matrons objected to the term "succussion" under the impression (mistaken, as it turned out) that it referred to an indelicate form of sexual congress.

SUDARIUM *n.* ❧ A cloth used for wiping sweat off the face, the most famous sudarium of all being the "vernicle," i.e., the veil or handkerchief of St. Veronica, believed to have retained miraculously the image of Christ's face when the saint wiped it for Him. "And now Edberg and Becker leave the court to change ends, and . . . heavens! Edberg has lost his sudarium!

This could be serious for the Swede, and . . . yes, Becker is offering Edberg the use of his own, but for some reason Edberg seems reluctant to accept it . . ."

SUPEREROGATION *n.* ❧ Superfluity; something over and above what is needed. "Works of supererogation" are good deeds over and above the call of duty. "Verily, Mallory, the midwife who brought you into the world performed a work of supererogation."

SUPERNACULUM *n.* ❧ A liquor of high quality, fit for drinking to the last drop. "It is a sad thing, Burnaby, that the custom of attending to one's religious devotions, upon arising in the morning and before retiring at night, has fallen into desuetude. In my own little way I try to compensate for that. I pride myself upon the fact that the sun does not rise upon a new day without my giving thanks with a supernaculum, in the privacy of my bedchamber."

SUPERNAL *a.* ❧ Coming from on high. "Supernal catch, lad!" you cry from your seat in the stand, as the outfielder just manages to pluck the ball out of the air. "Supernal catch!"

SYNCRETISTIC *a.* ❧ Seeking to identify common features of different belief systems, philosophies, or civilizations, and merge them into a single system. One can understand historians or theologians seeking to establish common elements in, for example, the Islamic, Judaic, and Christian traditions; but most modern historiographers would readily concede that no concept of syncretism can be considered sufficiently powerful to reconcile the existence of divine judgment with that of the television program *Candid Camera*.

## ❧ T ❧

**TABARD** *n.* ❧ A medieval sleeveless tunic or jacket. A suitable archaism, perhaps, for a T-shirt? "Do you have any Iron Maiden tabards?"

**TABESCENT** *a.* ❧ Wasting or withering away. (**TABEFACTION**: Emaciation.) Perhaps best used ironically, as with your Monday greeting for the bulimic co-worker who for many years has been growing more and more *globose* (q.v.).
"Glad to see that tabefaction has not set in
over the weekend, Leslie."

**TAPHEPHOBIA** *n.* ❧ Morbid dread of being buried alive. "No, not with you on top, Tabitha! I don't think I could handle that! I'm taphephobic, you see."

**TAPINOSIS** *n.* ❧ The use of degrading diction about a subject. To some extent facilitated, I regret to admit, by this book.

**TARDIGRADE** *a.* ❧ Slow in movement. "Hold it, children! That's a ladies' fashion boutique we've just passed; your mother has gone into tardigrade motion."

**TARSALGIA** *n.* ❧ Pain in the foot. Perhaps, using a little creative philology, you could refer to the person of your choice as an arsalgia.

**TARSORRHAPHY** *n.* ❧ Stitching the eyelids together. It is sometimes the sad duty of the lexicographer to record the almost-unthinkable. In the present case, some relief may perhaps be obtained from the realization that here we have the ultimate spelling test for the smug super-spellers in your home or office.

TAUROMACHIAN *a.* ❧ Of or pertaining to bullfights. "And are we to expect another tauromachian encounter when your mother visits us this Christmas, my dear?"

TEGESTOLOGIST *n.* ❧ A collector of beer coasters. The species is normally male, falls within the age range of 19 to 23, and certainly does not know that it is so called.

TELEOPHOBIA *n.* ❧ A morbid dread of definite plans. "I'm sorry, darling, but I have a medical problem that precludes any consideration of an actual marriage date. My teleophobia, I'm afraid—here's the doctor's certificate."

TELODYNAMIC *a.* ❧ Relating to the transmission of power over a long distance. "Telodynamics in action, darling; it's a long distance call from your mother."

TENEBRIFIC *a.* ❧ Making tenebrous, i.e., dark and obscure. "Gee whiz, your lectures are tenebrific, Professor! No—it's true, we all think so—really tenebrific!"

THERSITICAL *a.* ❧ Abusive and foul-mouthed. "I'd sooner you didn't bring the children this time, Gladys; if only I were as thersitical as they are I'd feel that I could relate to them better, but as it is . . ."

THIBLE *n.* ❧ (Pronounced "thibble.") A spatula. You could get real mileage out of this one if you ever found yourself dealing with an apothecary named Sybil.

THIGMOTAXIS *n.* ❧ The movement of an organism in response to an object providing a mechanical stimulus. "The cat's sleeping in my chair again, honey—pass me the broom and I'll try a little thigmotaxis."

THRASONICAL *a.* ❧ Bragging and boasting. "The test results are back, Mr. Wheelwright, and let me say at once that you have absolutely nothing to be thrasonical about."

THREMMATOLOGY *n.* ❧ The science of breeding domestic animals and plants. "She's given up on her husband and kids, I hear, and is into thremmatology now. Says it's more rewarding."

TIFFIN *n.* ❧ A snack or light lunch. Deflate your socially pacesetting friends who have just been carrying on about this delightful new Chinese restaurant that has the most amusing *yum cha,* by saying brightly: "Oh, that's a kind of tiffin, isn't it?"

TITUBATION *n.* ❧ A disorder in bodily equilibrium, causing an unsteady gait and trembling. You might ruefully admit to being a trifle titubant the morning after the night before.

TOMENTOSE *a.* ❧ Densely covered with down or matted hair. "For heaven's sake, Roger, get a haircut before you become totally tomentose."

TONITRUOUS *a.* ❧ Thundering, explosive. "And how are we tonight, my dear? Equanimitous or tonitruous?"

TORPILLAGE *n.* ❧ Electric shock therapy. "Why not try some alternative medicine, dearest, to see if that helps? A little homeopathy, perhaps, some iridology, a course of torpillage?"

TORREFY *v.* ❧ To parch or scorch; to dry with heat. Your wife's hair dryer might perhaps be referred to as a torrefier.

TRAGOMASCHALIA *n.* ❧ A condition in which the armpits are smelly. Fate has decreed that people with this condition always fall in love with people who are *nasute* (q.v.).

TREGETOUR *n.* ❧ A magician or juggler. In modern terms, a tax accountant.

TRISTILOQUY *n.* ❧ A dull and depressing speech. "And now, to really put a cap on the evening, we have the final speaker, one of our leading tristiloquists, Captain Arbuthnot . . ."

## ❧ U ❧

UBIETY *n.* ❧ The state of being in a definite place—of having location or, so to speak, "whereness." Another of those well-nigh inexplicable words. Who or what would not have ubiety? "This indefatigable ubiety of yours is a bit of a problem for us all, MacIndoe; could you manage to do something about it in the New Year?"

ULTRAFIDIAN *a.* ❧ Going beyond faith. "I suppose it would be ultrafidian to expect Lewis to arrive on time."

ULTRONEOUS *a.* ❧ Spontaneous. "Have you done the preliminary research for your ultroneous remarks at the Annual Dinner yet, Percival?"

UMBLES *n.* ❧ Entrails of an animal, more especially those of a deer, but extended to cover any that are typically consumed as food. Thence the expression "to eat humble pie," i.e., "umble pie," this being the fodder reserved for those at the lowest end of the table. You already knew that, of course; but it may not have occurred to you to foster the use of the term in other contexts. Thus "have some steak and umble (instead of kidney) pie," or "umbles (instead of liver) and bacon for breakfast today, dear," or, if you really want to lower the tone on a social occasion, "ah—my favorite—paté de umbles gras." Often consequential upon umbles are *wambles* (q.v.).

UMBO *n.* ❧ The knob on a toadstool cap, a shield, or a seashell. A nicely deflating term for one of those woolen beanies that your trendy friends adorn their sconces with as the skiing season approaches.

UNASINOUS *a.* ❧ Being equally stupid. "What a lovely marriage ceremony! So rare to see a couple so well-suited, so well-matched—so unasinous in every respect."

*Unasinous*

UNDERGROPE *v.* ❧ To conceive or understand. Readers may wish to devise their own exemplary uses for this term, but are advised to keep them to themselves.

UNDINISM *n.* ❧ The association of water with erotic thoughts. Statistics show a national incidence of one sufferer per household. Think about it—which member of *your* family spends longest in the shower?

UNGULATA *n.* ❧ The order of hoofed mammals. "Look out! Get the plastic carpet protectors down! Here comes the ungulata!" might well be the cry as you observe your young son's football team moving purposefully in the direction of the kitchen door after training.

UNTHIRLABLE *a.* ❧ Impenetrable. "Say no more old chap—your logic is unthirlable."

URTICANT *a.* ❧ Stinging (like a nettle). "Well, if you really need time out to 'consider our relationship,' as you so gracefully put it, why not go for a walk down the back paddock? It'll do you the world of good, too. Nice and urticant at this time of year!"

USUCAPTION *n.* ❧ The acquisition of property by right of long possession and enjoyment. Thus, in the average household, the bathroom is considered under common law to be owned, by right of usucaption, by the youngest female adult, and the telephone by the oldest female child.

UTRAQUIST *n.* ❧ One who partakes of the wine as well as the bread at communion. "So that settles what we're all having for entrée and main course. Now, what'll we have to drink? Any utraquists among us? No? Well, we won't be needing the wine list, waiter—just a carafe of house water, please."

UTTERANCE *n.* ❧ Great opportunity for a hidden double meaning here. Utterance of course means "saying," or "something said," but an archaic use of the term means "the bitter end," i.e., death, as in "fight to the utterance." "James, I can't tell you how much I look forward to your utterance."

# ❧ V ❧

**VALETUDINARIAN** *n.* ❧ An invalid—more especially one with a tendency to hypochondria. "No, I'm sorry, we don't want to discuss the Bible on our front doorstep with two perfect strangers; in any case we're both valetudinarians—so goodday to you . . . unless you'd care to make a donation?"

**VARIETIST** *n.* ❧ Someone whose attitudes or activities are not what most people would consider normal. Someone who chooses to be different. A recusant against the herd mentality, and to that extent the term is properly seen as complimentary. Thus, you are an eccentric; I am a varietist.

**VAVASOUR** *n.* ❧ One who held his lands of a tenant in chief, i.e., the small farmer who rented his plot from the big farmer who rented his plots from the lord of the manor, whose ancestors had stolen it all from someone. In modern terms, the student who boards in the backroom of the unit your daughter is renting. "I'll pay you back on Saturday week, Daddy, when my vavasour pays her rent for the month."

**VECORDIOUS** *a.* ❧ Crazy, senseless, lunatic. "No, darling, *of course* I'm quite happy for you to choose the color scheme. Just go ahead and trust your own judgment. I just know you can be relied on to come up with something utterly vecordious without any assistance from me."

**VENDITATION** *n.* ❧ Displaying as if for sale. "Have you seen the dress that our daughter is proposing to wear to the high school ball, dear? She seems to have graduated from ostentation to venditation."

VENTAGE *n.* ❧ A small outlet giving onto a confined space, as for example a fingerhole in some wind instruments. Just how far you go in applying this concept to the parts of the human body is up to you.

VENTOSENESS *n.* ❧ Flatulence; a tendency to suffer from wind. "Maurice, you take elevator no. 1—and remember, we're going to the eighteenth floor. Coralie, you'd better go with Maurice. Anyone else who's at all ventose? O.K., the rest of you come with me in elevator no. 2."

VERBICIDE *n.* ❧ That which kills words or their meanings, i.e., a development or circumstance that destroys the common usage for a particular word or phrase. The obvious example in modern times is "gay." Particularly unfortunate when, as in this case, the word so appropriated has a distinctive sense of its own and there are no obvious alternatives for that sense. So long, *Our Hearts Were Young and Gay*— you're history now.

VERECUND *a.* ❧ Modest, shy, or bashful. "O.K., stop the partying for just a moment while I make an announcement! Step forward, Dimity! Lower the lights and turn the spotlight on Dimity, someone! That's right—now, here's what you've all been waiting to hear—Dimity is . . . wait for it . . . verecund!"

VERISIMILITUDE *n.* ❧ The appearance of being true. The display of characteristics strongly suggestive of authenticity. Note that verisimilitude is not quite the same as *evidence* of truth; it stops short. "I concede, Baldwin, that this doctor's certificate lends, for the first time ever, I believe, a certain degree of verisimilitude to one of your sick-leave applications; but it would carry even more conviction if the handwriting was less legible and/or the word 'flu' was not spelled 'flew.'"

VERMIAN *a.* ✤ Wormlike. "Vermicular" means much the same, and "vermiculation" is a state of infestation by worms, or transformation into worms. (Think about it for a moment. Yes, there's a horror film concept somewhere in every dictionary.) "So you've been seeing her behind my back, you vermian little invertebrate . . ."

VERRUCOSE *a.* ✤ Covered in wartlike growths. Suitable for cursing under the guise of blessing. "Bon voyage, Jacinta; may your path be smooth, your mind ever active, and your hands ever verrucose."

VESPIARY *n.* ✤ A nest of wasps. Jacinta's reply: "May your workplace by day be as a humming hive, and in the evenings your house a vespiary."

VETUST *a.* ✤ Venerable from antiquity, like the author.

VEXILLOLOGIST *n.* ✤ A student of flags. One of those people who can, and do, tell you when the flag of Montenegro is being flown upside down, and why the green bar on the Bulgarian flag is exactly the same shade of green as that on the flag of the old Austro-Hungarian Empire. There are people like this, just as there are people who know all about medals and exactly how they should be worn. There are *psephologists* (q.v.) too.

VIBRISSA *n.* ✤ A hair in the nostril. "Well, bon voyage, Max; here's wishing you good health, a safe return, and lots and lots of vibrissae!"

VIDUITY *n.* ✤ Widowhood. "Well, Benson, if you're considering your financial future, now's the time to look at insurance as an investment option. For example, I'm sure your wife would appreciate what we call a nondeferred viduity . . ."

VILLEGGIATURA *n.* ❧ A rural extended holiday or retirement. The aspiration of the lexicographer. A good word, which, spoken aloud in a dreamy manner, is extremely conducive to mental health.

VISCEROTONIC *a.* ❧ Having an amiable, comfort-loving temperament of the kind normally associated with endomorphy. (An endomorph is a person who by physical type is soft, rounded, and fleshy, and by psychological type warm and sociable.) "Young gentleman wishes to meet viscerotonic millionairess; view comfort."

VITIATE *v.* ❧ To weaken, degrade, or spoil. "The impact of the Duke's address to the Conservation Society on the preservation of wildlife was somewhat vitiated by the circulation to members beforehand of a news report dealing with the great number of birds shot by the Duke during a sporting trip to the highlands."

VOMITORY *n.* ❧ In an ancient Roman amphitheater, the circumferential passage through which spectators reached the doors leading to the seating. The foyer to the dress circle, so to speak. As you display your home to a visitor, you could validly refer to the corridor between the children's bedrooms and the rec room as the vomitory.

## ❧ W ❧

WAMBLE *n.* ❧ A rumbling or similar disturbance of the stomach. A comforting word, which deserves to be more used. "Was that my wamble or yours?"

WAYZGOOSE *n.* ❧ A printer's annual holiday. My sources are silent on the matter of the timing of this holiday, but per-

*Whangdoodle*

sonal experience suggests that it is always taken on the day
when, had it not been taken, your job would
have been finished.

WEASINESS *n.* ❧ The quality or state of being given to
gluttony. Succeeds queasiness lexicographically, but
precedes it temporally.

WHANGDOODLE *n.* ❧ A mythical bird that grieves con-
tinuously. As far as the lexicographer can tell from the limited
source material available to him, this bears no relation to the
somewhat mystifying title of the classic Howlin' Wolf number
"Wang-dang-doodle," with its haunting refrain "We're gonna
pitch wang-dang-doodle all night long."

WHILOM *a.* or *adv.* ❧ Former(ly); once, erstwhile. A pleasant archaism to use once in a while, particularly when in the
company of those among your few remaining friends who are
most irritated by your penchant for the antediluvian. "Whilom,
when I was but a callow youth . . ."

WHIMLING *n.* ❧ A weak, childish person. Don't knock it—whimlings have a lot of fun while strong, adult persons are worrying.

WITZELSUCHT *n.* ❧ An emotional state characterized by futile attempts at humor. Too close for comfort, this one. Ten years I've been trying to win the Nobel Prize for Literature with these lousy definitions—even the BHP Award for Excellence, goddamit—even a Writer-in-Residence at a women's college in a small country town—anything—and what do I get? The Big O—and I'm not talking Roy Orbison here, I'm talking . . . [Editor's note: It would be kinder to draw a veil over the remainder of this quite lengthy, not to say rambling, item, which was the last one being worked on by Mr. Bowler before his unfortunate breakdown. Letters of encouragement, quantities of white chocolate, and negotiable bills of exchange may be sent to him by wellwishers, who are asked, however, in the interests of his ultimate recovery, not to include their own feeble attempts at humor in any covering letters.]

## ❧ X ❧

XANTHOPSIA *n.* ❧ An ophthalmic condition in which everything appears yellow. Condition of a person wearing dark glasses purchased from the "sale" section at the local gas station.

XENIUM *n.* ❧ A present given to a guest. (XENIAL: Pertaining to hospitality, or to the relationship between host and guest.) "Always nice to come to the Tennysons', isn't it? And I suppose it's not fair to expect a xenium these days—the old xenial customs have gone out the window, eh?"

XENODOCHEIONOLOGY *n.* ❧ Love of hotels and inns. A passion shared by drunkards, womanizers, and Upwardly Mobile Young Managers, to whom Visible Movement is more important than staying in the office and getting on with their work.

XENODOCHIUM *n.* ❧ A building for the reception of strangers; a caravanserai. Yes, this is it. The Superior Person's word for a motel.

XENOGENOUS *a.* ❧ Due to an outside cause. "*Most* impressed by your clever son's matriculation results, Ivy! Fancy you and Gavin bringing forth such a genius! Absolutely xenogenous!"

XYLOID *a.* ❧ Woody. "Little Robbie sure is his father's son, isn't he? Same happy smile, same hair color, same xyloid head . . ."

XYLOPYROGRAPHY *n.* ❧ Making designs on wood with a red-hot poker. Kids: use this word when your teachers ask you to fill in a career guidance form about what you want to do for a living. They won't have a dictionary that includes it, and they won't want to try to pronounce it in front of the class to ask you what it means. Make them suffer a little.

XYSTER *n.* ❧ A surgeon's instrument for scraping bones. "Well, Agatha, if you're sure the doctors can't find anything wrong with you, why not try a naturopath? And ask them to give you a good going over with a xyster. Does wonders for your circulation, I'm told."

# ❧ Y ❧

**YARBOROUGH** *n.* ❧ A hand of cards containing none higher than nine. If you ever get a hand with none *lower* than nine, you could always mutter something about bloody yarboroughs under your breath, on the off-chance that one of your opponents knows the term; and then, when the inevitable denouement occurs, exclaim that you never *could* remember whether it was higher or lower.

**YAUL** *v.* ❧ To deviate (in rocketry) from a stable course because of oscillation about the longitudinal axis. You *could* try this one on the traffic policeman, I suppose: "It's not what you think, Ossifer. I'm not drunk. I'm just suffering from yaul, and therefore deviating from a stable course because of oscillation about my longitudinal axis . . . "

**YESTERFANG** *n.* ❧ That which was taken at some time in the past. Your beloved's maidenhead; all the good seats in the grandstand; and the last bottle of really good champagne.

**YEULING** *n.* ❧ Walking around fruit trees praying for a good crop. Try it if you wish, but the author can only say that he has found swearing, abuse, and threats of extreme violence to be more effective.

# ❧ Z ❧

**ZEIGARNIK** *n.* ❧ A tendency to remember an uncompleted task. This is a term from the magic land of psychology, and describes a condition to which all of us are, to varying degrees, prone. With, of course, the notable exception of builders, who are immune.

ZEITGEIST *n.* ❧ The general intellectual, moral, and cultural level of an era. Thus, the zeitgeist of today's younger generation could be said to reflect the values of the conservation movement, equality of opportunity, the computer game, and the horror film.

ZELOTIPIA *n.* ❧ Morbid or fanatical zeal; jealousy. "It's great to see a family where both daughters play the piano. So good for the young people to have something like that, isn't it? Just see what it does for them—you can see the zelotipia shining in their eyes!"

ZENANA *n.* ❧ That part of an Indian house in which high-caste women were sequestered. "Mother, would you care to convey a message to my sister? She has retired to her bedroom in the usual high dudgeon, apparently in the belief that it is a zenana."

ZOILISM *n.* ❧ Carping, destructive criticism. "Ah, Miss Petherbridge, another solo from you on tonight's program, I see! If only I were free to convey to you the full extent of the zoilism that your playing inspires in me!"

ZOOERASTIA *n.* ❧ Sexual intercourse with an animal. As your office manager returns at the end of a lunch hour, red-faced and panting stertorously from the effects of his usual two-mile jog, you whisper to the new keyboard operator: "Don't ask—it's just his hobby—zooerastia. Couldn't handle that myself, but it seems to keep him fit." Sooner or later, she'll look it up.

ZOOPERY *n.* ❧ Experimentation on primitive animals. "Still having trouble with 3B, Carruthers? Try a little zoopery—tell them they can watch a pornographic video when they've mastered the subjunctive."

# Sources

The sources from which the words are derived include, as would be expected, various editions of the better-known dictionaries (more especially, Oxford, Webster's, Chambers, and Funk & Wagnalls) and also the following specific works:

Bombaugh, C. C. *Oddities and Curiosities of Words and Literature*. Dover, N.Y., 1961.

Byrne, Josefa Heifetz. *Mrs Byrne's Dictionary of Unusual, Obscure and Preposterous Words*. Citadel Press, Secaucus, N.J., 1976.

Drever, James. *A Dictionary of Psychology*. Penguin, London, 1958.

Haubrich, William S. *Medical Meanings: A Glossary of Word Origins*. Harcourt Brace Jovanovich, San Diego, 1984.

Hill, Robert H. (comp.). *A Dictionary of Difficult Words*. Signet, N.Y., 1975.

Johnson, Samuel. *A Dictionary of the English Language. Abstracted from the Folio Edition by the Author*. Allison et al., London, 1824.

Kupper, W. H. *Dictionary of Psychiatry and Psychology*. Colt Press, N.J., 1953.

Ogilvie, John (ed.). *A Supplement to the Imperial Dictionary: English, Technological and Scientific*. Blackie and Son, Glasgow, 1855.

Riley, P. A. and Cunningham, P. J. *The Faber Pocket Medical Dictionary*. Faber & Faber, London, 1977.

Shipley, Joseph T. *Dictionary of Word Origins*. Philosophical Library, N.Y., 1945.

*The Family Bible Dictionary*. Avenel Books, N.Y., n.d.

Tweney, C. F. and Hughes, L. E. C. (eds.). *Chambers Technical Dictionary,* Macmillan, N.Y., 1965.

Urdang, Laurence (ed.). *The New York Times Everyday Reader's Dictionary of Misunderstood, Misused, Mispronounced Words.* Weathervane Books, N.Y., nd.

Uvarov, E. B. and Chapman, D. R. *A Dictionary of Science.* Penguin, London, 1951.

Weekley, Ernest. *An Etymological Dictionary of Modern English.* Dover, N.Y., 1967.

*The Superior Person's Second Book of*
*Weird & Wondrous Words*

was set in Galliard, a typeface designed by Matthew Carter and introduced in 1978 by the Mergenthaler Linotype Company. Based on the types created by Robert Granjon in the sixteenth century, Galliard is the first of its genre to be designed exclusively for phototypesetting. A type of solid weight, it possesses authentic sparkle that is lacking in most current Garamonds. The italic is particularly felicitous and reaches back to the feeling of the chancery style, from which Claude Garamond's italic departed. Composition by NK Graphics, Keene, New Hampshire. Printed and bound by Maple-Vail Book Manufacturing Group, Binghamton, New York.